ESPECIALLY FOR

....

FROM

....

DATE

....

MINDFUL DEVOTIONS

FOR BUSY DAYS

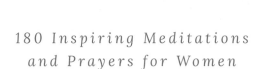

*180 Inspiring Meditations
and Prayers for Women*

DONNA K. MALTESE

BARBOUR
PUBLISHING

ISBN 978-1-63609-677-3
Adobe Digital Edition (.epub) 978-1-63609-767-1

Cover Design: Greg Jackson, Thinkpen Design

Published by Barbour Publishing, Inc., 1810 Barbour Drive, Uhrichsville, Ohio 44683, www.barbourbooks.com

Our mission is to inspire the world with the life-changing message of the Bible.

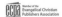

Printed in China.

INTRODUCTION

Our minds produce as many as 50,000 thoughts each day. That seems like an amazing number! But what's even more amazing is that approximately 80 percent of those thoughts are negative. How is a woman to defend herself against this dark and destructive onslaught in an already shadow-filled world? By immersing herself in the healing and protective powers of the Word of God.

Collected here are some of the most uplifting Bible verses you'll ever read, as well as a short devotion to inspire your heart and mind during the quiet moments of your busy day and a prayer to bring that day to completion. Read these pages in the morning to get your day started right. Or read them in the afternoon to give yourself a quick boost. Or read them at night before you go to sleep. Simply make a pledge to feed your soul with positive, inspiring thoughts, using this little book as a launching pad to a better outlook and *in*-look toward your life.

There's no better time to start than today. Just turn the page and see how God's Word can shed His light in your heart, soul, spirit, body, and mind. Now that's a positive!

THE CREATIVE ZONE

God created human beings; he created them godlike,
reflecting God's nature. He created them male and female.
GENESIS 1:27 MSG

Genesis 1 reveals God as the ultimate Creator. Because we were made in His image, we also love to create. It feeds something in us, deep down inside. When we are in that crafting mode, creating "new worlds," we lose all track of time. That's because we are doing what we were made to do—adding beauty to the world. Working with our hands and minds, we are all artists, whether we are creating meals, knitting sweaters, or arranging flowers. For all the beauty we mold and shape is an expression and a reflection of the ultimate Creator God, not only working His way through us, but also looking back at us—and liking what He sees.

Thank You, Lord, for Your wonderful creation. Help me imitate
Your artistry by adding beauty to the world. Work through
me, using my hands and mind to Your delight. Then smile
down upon me, pleased with what You, my Creator, see.

GOD REMEMBERS

*But God remembered Noah and all the wild animals and
the livestock that were with him in the ark, and he sent
a wind over the earth, and the waters receded.*

<small>GENESIS 8:1 NIV</small>

In the midst of our troubles, we may sometimes get the feeling that God has forgotten about us. Exhausted from sleepless, stormy nights, muscles strained from trying to hold on to the sides of a violently rocking boat, we moan and groan, asking, "God, are You there?"

Yet we need not fret. God always knows exactly what's happening in our lives. We need only have faith that He is with us before, during, and after the storms, knowing He will not only rescue us from deep waters but set us upon dry land as troublesome waters recede.

---

*God, I know You are here with me, loving me,
lighting my way. I know You go before me,
walk beside me, hover above me, and protect me
from behind. Thank You for being a continual
presence in my life, breath by breath.*

THE GOD OF POSSIBILITIES

Is anything too hard or too wonderful for the Lord?
Genesis 18:14 ampc

There is no use putting limits on a limitless God! He can do *anything*—and *everything*! God can give a childless couple, past the age of childbearing, a brand-new, natural-born son. He can make a dry path through the sea. He can make the sun stand still. He can turn sorrow into joy, water into wine, and death into life. So why keep yourself from believing the impossible? Look to God. He has no limits. And as a daughter of God, neither do you. Keep your dreams alive, knowing God is the God of possibilities. There is nothing too hard or too wonderful for Him.

I can't help but smile, Lord, knowing that You are the God of possibilities. Because I am confident that You have no limits, my heart bursts with what might be. Knowing You can find a way to make my dreams come true gives me new hope.

AN OUTSTRETCHED HAND

Lot's wife looked back, and she became a pillar of salt.
GENESIS 19:26 NIV

It's simple. When we keep looking back to what once was, we do one of two things: We turn into a pillar of salt, grounded where we stand. Or, we trip up because our eyes aren't on the path ahead of us but upon what we've left behind.

So the only really viable solution is for us to allow God and His angels to get a good grip on us and hurry us out of the past. With our hands in theirs and our eyes on the path ahead, we will quickly find ourselves in a better place. All it takes is a willing heart, an outstretched hand, and faith in the one who is wiser than us.

With a willing heart and outstretched hand, I reach for You, Lord. May Your angels whisk me from the past and into the present, where I can focus on Your loving face. Pull me from what was, and place my feet on what is.

FORMULA FOR SUCCESS

O Lord, God of my master Abraham, I pray You,
cause me to meet with good success today,
and show kindness to my master Abraham.
GENESIS 24:12 AMPC

Before sending his servant to seek a bride for his son Isaac, Abraham told his servant, "The Lord, in Whose presence I walk [habitually], will send His Angel with you and prosper your way" (verse 40 AMPC). In so saying, Abraham planted in his servant a seed of truth, faith, and optimism from the outset. Later, the servant prayed his own prayer in Genesis 24:12. When this prayer was answered, as foretold and believed, the servant immediately "bowed down. . .and worshiped the Lord" (verse 26 AMP). This is a wonderful formula for any of God's servants to follow: envision success, pray for success, then worship when success is obtained.

Lord, thank You for sending Your angel ahead of me
to prosper me in my way. Prompt me to follow where
he leads, then fill my mind's eye with a vision of success,
and remind me to worship You when that success is realized.

IT'S ALL GOOD

Joseph said to them, "Do not be afraid, for am I in the
place of God? But as for you, you meant evil against
me; but God meant it for good, in order to bring it
about as it is this day, to save many people alive."
GENESIS 50:19–20 NKJV

Sometimes the unexpected happens: we are betrayed by loved ones, falsely accused by strangers, and discarded by society. The good thing about it is that no matter what happens to us, God means it for good. So there's no need to fret, seek revenge, or bad-mouth those who have hurt us. Instead, just continue hanging with the Lord. Have faith that He—the King on the throne and the one and only judge—knows what He's doing. And it's all good.

Help me remember that You, Lord, can make good come
out of any situation I may face. Remind me each day that
You know what You're doing in my life—and it's all good.
All that's left for me to do is praise Your holy name.

A HARD PLACE

Moses told the people, Fear not; stand still (firm, confident, undismayed) and see the salvation of the Lord which He will work for you today. For the Egyptians you have seen today you shall never see again. The Lord will fight for you, and you shall hold your peace and remain at rest.
EXODUS 14:13–14 AMPC

Just when you feel trapped between the proverbial rock and a hard place, turn to God. He will find a way out you never dreamed of or imagined. All you need to do is stand firm. The troubles that have come upon you today you will never see again in quite the same way. So, rest easy, no matter what is happening in your life. God will part any sea that you need to get through.

I am confident in the fact that no matter what comes against me today, I don't need to worry or be afraid. For You, Lord, are beside me, ready to fight for me. All I need to do is stand firm in my faith and rest in Your peace.

GOD'S PERSPECTIVE

"You have seen what I did to the Egyptians. You know how I carried you on eagles' wings and brought you to myself."
EXODUS 19:4 NLT

What a great visual. Imagine God as a great eagle, carrying you out of all of your doubts, worries, fears. On His wings, you rise above all the pettiness, pressure, and pains of this world. He swiftly brings you into His presence. There, safe, warm, secure, nothing matters but you and God. You look back down on earth and suddenly see all things through God's perspective. The mountains of obstacles you'd encountered on earth seem very small from this heavenly height. With a new perspective, you return, knowing what once seemed impossible to scale is actually an effortless climb.

Upon Your great and powerful wings, Lord, I soar above my doubts, worries, and fears. In Your presence I find rest and safety. From this height, all my earthly problems—all those mountains of obstacles—become molehills. With You, I am able to overcome.

GOD'S ALREADY BEEN

*"See, I am sending an angel before you to protect you on your
journey and lead you safely to the place I have prepared for
you. Pay close attention to him, and obey his instructions."*
EXODUS 23:20–21 NLT

Wherever you're headed, God's already been. He's got everything
all set up. The beds are made, the fridge stocked. Your favorite
book is next to a cushy chair, and your own special music is play-
ing in the background. And God's already sent His angel ahead
of you to lead and protect you on your journey. All you need to
do is get there. Are you paying close attention to God and His
angel, obeying His instructions, walking where He wants you to
step? Remember: With God, obedience is the only surefire way to
travel.

*What joy I find in knowing You've already been to where
I'm headed, Lord! You've already scoped everything out.
You've sent your angel to lead and protect me. Open my
eyes, Lord, to where You would have me place my feet
so that each moment, I am one step closer to You!*

YOUR PERSONAL GOD

"I'll set up my residence in your neighborhood; I won't avoid or shun you; I'll stroll through your streets. I'll be your God; you'll be my people. I am GOD, your personal God who rescued you."

LEVITICUS 26:11–12 MSG

Could you imagine God moving in next door to you and walking down your streets, jazzed to be so near to the one whom He has rescued? Sounds amazing, right? But the fact is, God's already with you every minute of every day. He resides not just in your neighborhood but actually within *you*—and within all others He has rescued! All the power of His love, encouragement, and forgiveness is already inside of you. It doesn't get any more personal and empowering than that.

I'm stunned and fascinated with this concept—the truth that You are not just beside me but within me, Lord. . .as well as in all other believers who walk the same road I do! Thank You, God, for the love, encouragement, and forgiveness that already reside within me. . .within You.

WELL ABLE

Then Caleb quieted the people before Moses,
and said, "Let us go up at once and take possession,
for we are well able to overcome it."
NUMBERS 13:30 NKJV

Sometimes we cower in fear of the obstacles before us. Our imaginations take hold, making mountains out of molehills, monsters out of shadows. But then we remember God. We call to mind the idea that nothing can defeat Him. With God on our side, nothing can stand before us—no mountains, monsters, lions, leviathans, or Goliaths. We, like a courageous Caleb, can quiet our thoughts by saying—and believing—"I will go up at once and take possession of this situation, for I am well able to conquer it." Such words will transport us out of the shadow lands and into the sun of the Promised Land.

Thank You, Lord, for being by and on my side. Your presence assures me that nothing can shake me. In this moment, I quiet all my doubts and fears by saying—and believing—"I will go up and take possession of this situation, for I am well able to conquer it!"

IT'S ALL IN HOW
YOU LOOK AT IT

*And Moses made a serpent of bronze and put
it on a pole, and if a serpent had bitten any man,
when he looked to the serpent of bronze [attentively,
expectantly, with a steady and absorbing gaze], he lived.*
NUMBERS 21:9 AMPC

God wants our full attention on Him. Not just a quick glance, hoping He really doesn't notice us. Nor does He want us fearing that, when He does detect us, He may ask us to do something that, on the surface, seems impossible for us to do. With God, we are to have no fear. He wants our eyes on Him, "attentively, expectantly, with a steady and absorbing gaze." For that is the only firm focus on God that will truly save. So, today, do an about-face. Eyes front. Allow an eager focus on your Father to banish all your fears.

With eyes closed, I look into Your face, Lord, full of expectancy, attentively searching Your countenance for the light that radiates from Your presence. Focused on You, my fears disappear. My worries dissipate. Eyes on You, I know all is and all will be well.

GOD'S PROMISES

"God is not a man, that He should lie, nor a son of man,
that He should repent; has He said, and will He not do
it? Or has He spoken, and will He not make it good?"

NUMBERS 23:19 NASB

God's Word is chock-full of promises for every believer. Since God does not lie, each and every one of those promises will hold true. Not just yesterday. Not just today—but tomorrow and all the days after that. What God has spoken, He will make come to pass. So shore up your faith by claiming each and every one of His assurances, knowing there is no limit to the promise fulfillment of a limitless God. What He did for Sarah, Hannah, Rahab, Naomi, Deborah, Abigail, Elizabeth, Mary, Lois, Eunice, and Dorcas, He will do for you—and so much more.

You're as good as Your Word, Lord. Knowing this truth,
I take Your assurances as my reality, my light, and my
guide. I claim all that You've promised to the women
who have gone before me, with confidence, hope, and
expectation that what You have spoken will come true.

YOUR ENTIRE BEING

And now, Israel, what does the Lord your God require of you
but [reverently] to fear the Lord your God, [that is] to walk in
all His ways, and to love Him, and to serve the Lord your God
with all your [mind and] heart and with your entire being.

DEUTERONOMY 10:12 AMPC

"Your entire being." That's what God wants. No halfway devotion. No mere lip service. But you—heart, mind, body, soul—every ounce of you walking in His ways, loving Him, and serving Him. That means spending good quality time in His presence. Really listening for His voice. And then actually obeying Him, going where He wants you to go. Wouldn't you want your own child to do the same?

Be with me today, Lord, as I endeavor to walk in Your ways,
to love You above all else, to serve You with my entire heart, mind,
body, and soul. Spirit to spirit, I follow. Lead me, Lord. Lead on.

REAL TRUTH

It is the Lord Who goes before you; He will [march] with you;
He will not fail you or let you go or forsake you; [let there be no
cowardice or flinching, but] fear not, neither become broken
[in spirit—depressed, dismayed, and unnerved with alarm].
DEUTERONOMY 31:8 AMPC

It is easy to get distracted by the news. In fact, the words "depressed, dismayed, and unnerved with alarm" pretty well describe someone who has just watched the eleven o'clock newscast. But here's the thing—God's Word can wipe out all those emotions. A dive into Psalms can calm that palpitating heart. Some wisdom from Proverbs can soothe your nerves. How do you spell *relief*? GOD'S WORD. The real truth to live by—an anchor for the soul! Now that's deep!

When despair weighs me down, Lord, help me to not lose myself
in the darkness it brings and instead dive into the light of Your
Word. Soothe my frayed nerves with the peace of Your psalms.
Let me know there is always hope and joy to be found in You.

STRENGTH FOR TODAY

"As your days, so shall your strength be. There is no one like the God of Jeshurun, who rides the heavens to help you. . . . The eternal God is your refuge, and underneath are the everlasting arms."

DEUTERONOMY 33:25–27 NKJV

No matter what you have to do today, relax. God will give you the strength to do it! He will ride to your side to help you. He always has been, is now, and always will be around to help you. He will not only protect you but fight for you. Just allow God's strength and power to work its magic. He's got you covered—today and tomorrow. So no matter how the situation looks, God is with you, upholding you and giving you the strength to face whatever may come.

Earthly sights are not my reality, Lord, nor are the imaginings of my heart. No matter what comes my way, I turn to You for the truth of the matter. I allow Your Spirit to envelop mine. Knowing You are with me, upholding me, I find the strength to face anything.

MAKE YOUR WAY

This Book of the Law shall not depart out of your mouth,
but you shall meditate on it day and night, that you
may observe and do according to all that is written in
it. For then you shall make your way prosperous, and
then you shall deal wisely and have good success.
JOSHUA 1:8 AMPC

Because so many things in this society are vying for our attention, we can end up getting far off track. One way to keep ourselves spiritually fit and focused is to meditate, optimally daily, on God's Word. Find a Bible verse that nourishes your spirit. Write it out, then speak it onto your heart. Allow its words and meaning to take root in you. Fulfill it in your life. Then, and only then, will you have prosperity, wisdom, and success. That's a promise.

Shine Your light into Your Word today, Lord. Show me
what You would have me speak into my heart, write upon
my mind, and plant deep within my spirit. For only by
breathing and living in Your wisdom will I find true success.

NEVER ALONE

*"Have I not commanded you? Be strong and of
good courage; do not be afraid, nor be dismayed,
for the LORD your God is with you wherever you go."*
JOSHUA 1:9 NKJV

In the first chapter of Joshua, God tells Joshua to be strong and
courageous. He says this a total of four times! Apparently God was
trying to get a very important point across: because He is with
us wherever we go, we *must* be strong and brave! And that's an
order! So take heart, woman of strength and courage. You are
never flying solo, no matter how detached from the rest of the
world you may sometimes feel. Your pilot and navigator God is
with you—whenever and wherever you go. No parachute needed.

---

*I'm ready to soar with You, Lord. With You as my pilot,
I find the strength and courage to do all that You
call me to do, to go where You direct me to go,
to be the woman You designed me to be!*

THE GREATEST ROLE

Now Deborah, a prophetess, the wife of Lapidoth,
was judging Israel at that time.
JUDGES 4:4 NKJV

Women assume many different roles at different stages of their lives. We go from being daughters to students to graduates to career women to wives to mothers to grandmothers, and so on. With all those individual roles come many different hats, enough to sometimes drive you crazy. It's nice to know that back in the "old days," Deborah also assumed many different roles, including the "mother in Israel" (Judges 5:7 AMPC). Yet the most supreme role she and we will *ever* play is that of being a daughter of God, the Most High King. Focusing on that role will give us the greatest wisdom and satisfaction in life.

I play many different roles in this life, Lord. Yet the original role You assigned me is that of Your daughter, Most High King. You have made me a princess, one who seeks Your wisdom, light, and love. O Sovereign of my heart, lead on.

MIGHTY HEROINE

The angel of the Lord appeared to him and said,
"Mighty hero, the Lord is with you!"

JUDGES 6:12 NLT

When God went to see Gideon, He called him a "mighty hero"—
and this was before Gideon had done any kind of fighting or rescuing. In fact, in verse 15, Gideon asks God how he, Gideon, will
be able to save Israel since his clan is the poorest in his neighborhood and he is the least in his own father's house! Amazingly
enough, God saw something heroic in Gideon that Gideon had yet to
reveal. So take heart. You, woman of strength, courage, and valor,
are more than meets *your* eye! Grab hold of that truth and the
added knowledge that *with God*, you can be and do anything!

You have made me more than meets the eye, Lord. You see
me as a woman of strength, courage, and valor. Help me
to live that reality, Lord. Help me to become—and to
see myself as—the mighty heroine You created me to be!

A FORK IN THE ROAD

Ruth replied...."Wherever you go, I will go;
wherever you live, I will live. Your people will
be my people, and your God will be my God."
RUTH 1:16 NLT

Both Orpah and Ruth began to follow their mother-in-law, Naomi, as she started her journey back to Israel. But only one stuck with her to the end—Ruth. How many times do you turn around after Christ has led you to a fork in the road? Ask yourself: "Am I willing to go wherever Jesus takes me, to live where He lives? Are His people my people, His God my God, His Father my Father?"

Need to make a decision, to choose a direction? No problem. Gather up all your belongings and head down the road with Jesus. Choose to stick with Him—no matter what—and you'll always find yourself going the right way.

No matter what road comes to meet me, Lord, I will follow
You. For You alone will lead me the right way. You are my
Savior, my brother, my Lord, and my friend. Your people are
my people...Your Father, my Father. Lead on, Lord, lead on.

A WOMAN OF STRENGTH

And now, my daughter, fear not. I will do for you all you require, for all my people in the city know that you are a woman of strength (worth, bravery, capability).

RUTH 3:11 AMPC

It takes lots of strength to leave all you are familiar with and go to a strange place, somewhere way out of your comfort zone, to stick your neck out in an effort to provide for yourself and others. Yet when you do move out with unshakable commitment and faith, people notice your bravery, your capability. Even better than that, God rewards you for your efforts. So simply have courage as you continually seek His protection, and stay unwaveringly close to Him as His blessings unfold for you; for you too are a woman of His strength.

In You, Lord, I have an unshakable commitment and faith. Knowing You are always with me, that I am flying high beneath Your protective wing, unwaveringly close to You, I find the courage and capability to do all that You ask. In You I become a woman of strength.

ALL AGLOW

Hannah was speaking in her heart; only her
lips moved but her voice was not heard.
1 SAMUEL 1:13 AMPC

A tearful, childless Hannah poured out her heart to God, asking for a son. When the priest Eli noticed her, he thought she was drunk. After she corrected this false impression, he prayed that God would answer her prayer. Then she walked away, "her face radiant" (1 Samuel 1:18 MSG).

Although God can read your mind, He still wants to hear what you have to say. Take some time to consider the desire God has planted in your life. Then tell Him all about it, knowing He is bound to fulfill your dream. Afterward, as you rise from your knees, you too will find yourself glowing.

Lord, open my heart to the desire You have planted within
me. Help me to speak that desire back to You. Then walk
with me as I seek what You have already planned. Open my
eyes to the boundless opportunities You set before me.

EARS WIDE OPEN

Then GOD came and stood before him exactly as before,
calling out, "Samuel! Samuel!" Samuel answered,
"Speak. I'm your servant, ready to listen."
1 SAMUEL 3:10 MSG

Could you imagine God standing in front of you, calling out your name? Would such a startling event leave you absolutely tongue-tied? Yet God is speaking to you each and every day. When you open up His Word or listen to a sermon, it's as if God is standing right there, calling your name! Are you paying attention? Listen up, ladies. God's looking for a few good women. Let Him know you're available. Tell Him, "Speak. I'm Your servant, ready to listen." When you're in tune with God, when your ears, arms, and heart open wide to His call, miracles abound.

Lord, my ears, arms, and heart are open to Your call.
Speak, for I am listening with all my being. Tell me all
that's on Your mind. Guide me with Your Word. Lead me on
the path You have prepared for me—a path rife with miracles.

WHAT REALLY COUNTS

*GOD told Samuel, "Looks aren't everything. Don't be impressed
with his looks and stature. I've already eliminated him.
GOD judges persons differently than humans do. Men and
women look at the face; GOD looks into the heart."*

1 SAMUEL 16:7 MSG

Have you ever met someone who appeared to be beautiful—and
then she spoke, her words marring whatever presentation she'd
been trying to make? The old adage is true: beauty *is* only skin
deep. So, it would behoove us to spend less time fighting physical fat and wrinkles and more time seeking spiritual God's form
and face. With His presence developing deep within you, you'll
find yourself shining with His light and reflecting His perfect
love. That's a beautification process to die for!

*True beauty is in the light You plant within me, Lord—
the light that comes from living in Your Word,
from soaking up Your presence, from leaning into
Your grace. May I be one who reflects Your light,
making this world ever brighter and ever blessed.*

OVER AND OVER AGAIN

The Lord Who delivered me out of the paw of
the lion and out of the paw of the bear, He will
deliver me out of the hand of this Philistine.
1 SAMUEL 17:37 AMPC

God has saved you over and over again. First, helping you to rise above small challenges, then bigger ones. Thus there is no need to fear any new or bigger giants that may come your way. If God has saved you once, you can be confident He will be there for you again and again. And there's no need to arm yourself with a sling and some stones. You don't need them—for God is ready, willing, and able to not only deliver you but to fight the battle for you, over and over again.

Lord, thank You for continually delivering me from the threats—
seen and unseen—that come against me. With You by my side,
I am confident in Your constant protection, Your unparalleled
love, Your ability to vanquish what I, in my own power, cannot.

NEVERTHELESS

*And the king and his men went to Jerusalem against the Jebusites,
the inhabitants of the land, who spoke to David, saying, "You
shall not come in here; but the blind and the lame will repel
you," thinking, "David cannot come in here." Nevertheless
David took the stronghold of Zion (that is, the City of David).*
2 SAMUEL 5:6–7 NKJV

David had a good habit of not listening to naysayers. His brothers
and Saul told him that he, a boy shepherd, couldn't kill a giant.
Now here were people telling David he couldn't take their city.
"Nevertheless" he did! When you are faced with discouragers,
giants, and strongholds, turn your back to them and grab hold
of your own "nevertheless," knowing that with God all things are
possible.

---

*You, Lord, are my "nevertheless" God. When others
say I can't do something or that I am powerless, I will
nevertheless do the impossible. Because with You by
my side, countless miracles can—and will—happen!*

YOUR SHINING KNIGHT

*GOD is bedrock under my feet, the castle in which I live,
my rescuing knight. My God—the high crag where I
run for dear life, hiding behind the boulders, safe in
the granite hideout; my mountaintop refuge.*

2 SAMUEL 22:2–3 MSG

How wonderful to have a refuge in which to hide, a place where you know you are safe, where you will be looked after. God, like a knight, is here to save you from all harm, ready to sweep you up out of the swamp of trouble and carry you off! Although they can bring you comfort, there's no need to run to friends or family. Instead, it is better to run to the one who no one can defeat—your shining knight, the almighty Lord, your all-powerful Father, the King, your Savior.

---

*Upon You alone I depend, Lord. For You are the rock upon which
I stand, the keeper of my castle, the knight who continually
rescues me. With You in my life, standing by my side, working
deep within me, I know I am safe, secure, and well protected.*

PROMISES SPOKEN
AND FULFILLED

*O Lord, the God of Israel, there is no God like You in heaven
above or on earth beneath, keeping covenant and showing
mercy and loving-kindness to Your servants who walk before
You with all their heart. You have kept what You promised
Your servant David my father. You also spoke with Your
mouth and have fulfilled it with Your hand, as it is this day.*
1 KINGS 8:23–24 AMPC

When we wholeheartedly follow God, His words come true in our
lives. He's not just talk. He actually moves mountains to keep His
promises to us. When He speaks, it happens. So, need a lift? Go to
the Word, find a promise that speaks to your heart, believe it, and
know that as you walk before your God, your eyes fixed on Him,
that promise will become a reality.

---

*As I enter Your Word, Lord, reveal the promise You have
prepared for me—one that speaks to my heart and into my
life. Today I claim that promise, that vow You have made,
assured it will transform into and become my reality.*

TENDER CARE

The angel of the LORD came back a second time and
touched him and said, "Get up and eat, for the journey
is too much for you." So he got up and ate and drank.
1 KINGS 19:7–8 NIV

Elijah was on the run—literally. He was desperately trying to escape the evil Jezebel. Finally, exhausted and depressed, he stopped and sat under a tree, praying that he might die. What did God do? He didn't yell. He didn't lecture. He took care of His servant. He provided Elijah with food and rest. Once God renewed Elijah physically, He restored His servant mentally, emotionally, and spiritually until he could take up his mantle again, a stronger person than before.

Tired of running? Need a break? Go to God. Rest and restore yourself in Him. No one will care for you as tenderly as He.

Lord, help me to find my rest in You. As I close my eyes and
imagine Your presence with me, I lean back against Your chest,
changing the rhythm of my breath to match Yours. Cocooned in
Your arms, I find the peace I need and the tenderness I crave.

SPIRITUAL FLIERS

Suddenly a chariot and horses of fire came
between them [Elijah and Elisha] and Elijah
went up in a whirlwind to heaven.
2 KINGS 2:11–12 MSG

Would that we could, at times, be beamed up by God—up and away from problems, challenges, and heartaches. Yet that's just what can happen, figuratively speaking. By lifting our hearts, souls, minds, and spirits up to God, we *can* rise above all the sorrows of this life. Whisked into His presence, we discover the kingdom of God within, and so obtain not only His compassion and courage but also His peace and perspective of this world. And the best part is that the more we rack up those spiritual frequent-flier miles, the more contented with all things we become.

Beam me up, Lord! Whisk me away from this earth
and into Your heavenly presence. Lift me far above
the heartaches, troubles, and challenges of this world.
Cover me with Your compassion and courage. Impart
Your peace upon me. Court me within Your kingdom.

OPEN EYES

"Don't be afraid.... Those who are with us are more than those who are with them." And Elisha prayed, "Open his eyes, LORD, so that he may see." Then the LORD opened the servant's eyes, and he looked and saw the hills full of horses and chariots of fire all around Elisha.

2 KINGS 6:16–17 NIV

When troubles and fears come our way, we sometimes have limited vision. We see only the physical, and so our eyesight is limited to the standard 20/20. But if we pray and ask God to open our spiritual eyes as well, we will see His working in our lives, which may just include a multitude of horses and chariots of fire coming to our rescue.

Lord, open my spiritual eyes. Show me where You are working in my life. Give me a different perspective—Your perspective— in my situation. Remind me that You and Your angels, Your horses and chariots, surround me and will rescue and protect me.

COMMITTED CONFIDENCE

The field commander said to them, "Tell Hezekiah:
'This is what the great king, the king of Assyria, says:
On what are you basing this confidence of yours?'"

2 KINGS 18:19 NIV

No matter what, King Hezekiah clung to God. He never stopped following Him. Because of that, "the LORD was with him; he was successful in whatever he undertook" (verse 7 NIV). This gave Hezekiah the confidence to keep out the Assyrian army when it came knocking on the Jerusalem wall. After Hezekiah's passion-filled prayer, which ended with "LORD our God, deliver us from his hand, so that all the kingdoms of the earth may know that you alone, LORD, are God" (2 Kings 19:19 NIV), the angel of the Lord wiped out 185,000 of the enemy. Victory comes to the woman who clings not to people or possessions but commits all to her confidence in God.

Lord, You know me. I am a woman of Your world. I cling to You. You alone are my hope and confidence, my master and protector, my provider and rescuer. You alone are my God.

THE BIG BREAKTHROUGH

*So [Israel] came up to Baal-perazim, and David smote
[the Philistines] there. Then David said, God has
broken my enemies by my hand, like the bursting
forth of waters. Therefore they called the name of
that place Baal-perazim [Lord of breaking through].*
1 CHRONICLES 14:11 AMPC

With its force and power, water can form grand canyons, sweep houses away, redefine a coastline. Yet God is even more powerful. Our God is a God of breakthroughs. With one swipe of His hand, He can upend our problems, give us peace amid chaos, break through barriers, bring down walls we, by ourselves, could never move. So never give up. Never surrender. Your "Lord of breaking through" is on His way, and your path will soon be clear!

---

*God, You are the Lord of breakthroughs. There's no problem
You can't solve, no divide You can't bridge, no chaos You
can't calm. Because You're in my life, I don't ever need to
surrender. So I pray You would clear a pathway, lead me
on, and help me break through the barrier before me.*

AN ACTIVE FAITH

Search for the LORD and for his strength;
continually seek him.

1 CHRONICLES 16:11 NLT

What power those words contain. How amazing it would be to live each moment of each day seeking and searching for God and His strength. What's even more amazing is that King David sang these words after the ark of God was brought into Jerusalem. Thus, even though the presence of God was within his walls, David still told his people to continually look for God. That's an active faith. A doing faith. A walking faith. Although God is within your heart, continually search for Him and His strength—around every corner, down every road, in every step. Seek God always—and in all ways—and you will be amazed at what you find.

Lord, I love the idea of having an active faith, a "doing"
faith, a "walking" faith. Every day, may I search for
You, Your strength, Your way, Your power... May I
see You around every corner, down every path, along
every byway... As I seek You, may I find You, Lord.

ON THE LOOKOUT

"You asked GOD for help and he gave you the victory.
GOD is always on the alert, constantly on the lookout for
people who are totally committed to him. You were foolish
to go for human help when you could have had God's help.
Now you're in trouble—one round of war after another."
2 CHRONICLES 16:9 MSG

For one battle, King Asa asked God for help—and experienced victory. For the next fight, he went to a *human* ruler for help—and lost. It's amazing how, even after God has worked major victories in our lives, we so often trust in people and things other than Him to help us, time and time again. For sure and consistent victories, lean on the solid Rock of Ages, not a permeable piece of shale. Remember, God's always looking for those totally dependent on Him.

My dear and loving Rock of Ages, I lean upon You in every
challenge, and I trust in You for every victory. You are
the solid rock beneath my feet as I stand firm in my faith.
I depend upon You alone. . .and in You alone, I live.

RIVETED

We have no might to stand against this great company that is coming against us. We do not know what to do, but our eyes are upon You.

2 CHRONICLES 20:12 AMPC

King Jehoshaphat knew a huge army was coming his way. At first, he was frightened, but then he "set himself [determinedly, as his vital need] to seek the Lord" (verse 3 AMP). In public prayer, Jehoshaphat bravely admitted to his people that he didn't know what to do. Yet that kind of public (or private) confession is just what God wants to hear. It's okay not knowing what to do. And it's even more okay to admit it. When we bow in humility and helplessness to God, He raises us up in strength and victory because our eyes are riveted on Him.

I have no idea what to do, Lord. I don't know how to face the challenge before me. So I bow before You in this moment, asking You to rise up on my behalf. I fix my eyes on You, knowing You will bring strength and victory to my situation!

A PROMPT TO PRAISE

You shall not need to fight in this battle; take your positions,
stand still, and see the deliverance of the Lord [Who
is] with you. . . . Fear not nor be dismayed. Tomorrow
go out against them, for the Lord is with you.
2 CHRONICLES 20:17 AMPC

Knowing God is with us and will fight our battles is a major relief! Why, with Him in our camp, there's no way we can lose! This kind of assurance, applied on a regular basis, will prevent stress, physical aches and pains, and depression. Just taking our positions and standing still—doing what we can and confidently leaving the rest up to God—is not only a wonderful remedy for what ails us, but an attitude that will prompt us to praise. And, just like Jehoshaphat's people, amid that praise, we will prosper and realize victory.

You have told me, Lord, that You are with me, standing beside me.
And so, I will neither fear nor be discouraged. Instead, I will take
up my position and be still, looking for You to deliver me from
whatever comes against me. And to You I will sing my praises!

A HEART FOR GOD'S WORD

For Ezra had prepared and set his heart to
seek the Law of the Lord [to inquire for it
and of it, to require and yearn for it].

EZRA 7:10 AMPC

Ezra was determined to eke out every last meaning of God's Word, to understand it and apply it to his life. Our study of God's Word should not feel like a chore. It should be something we crave. It should be as vital to us as the air we breathe, the water we drink, the food we eat. It should be our shelter, our clothing, our refuge. Ezra set his heart to seek God's Word and went on to lift a nation out of the abyss and back to God. Dedicated women of the way can do the same.

Lord, I hunger for Your Word. Help me understand it and
apply it to my life as I open Your Book and drink in what
You rain upon my heart, spirit, soul, and mind. May I
daily set my heart to seek all Your Word has to offer.

STRONG HANDS
FOR GREAT FEATS

*They all wanted to frighten us, thinking, Their
hands will be so weak that the work will not be
done. But now strengthen my hands!*

NEHEMIAH 6:9 AMPC

Nehemiah refused to be frightened and discouraged when challenged with rebuilding and repairing the wall and gates of Jerusalem. Instead of listening to enemies and naysayers, Nehemiah prayed for God to strengthen his hands, to help him and the people do the work he knew God wanted them to do. The result? The wall was finished in just fifty-two days!

In order to accomplish a mighty feat, you too can pray with all your heart, "God, now strengthen my hands!" In so doing, you'll not only get naysayers out of your head but astound them with your efforts.

---

*Lord, I pray with all my heart, mind, and soul that You would
strengthen my hands and enlighten my spirit so I can do
the work You have created me to do. Thank You, Lord!*

YOUR CERTAIN PLACE

"Who knows but that you have come to your
royal position for such a time as this?"

ESTHER 4:14 NIV

All who believe in Jesus are daughters of a King. Thus, if you believe, you are a royal princess! Pretty cool! But with that position comes some obligation. God has set you in a certain family, a place of employment, church, school group—any number of areas. And who knows but that you have been born at this time and in this place, in this royal position as a daughter of a King, to do something extraordinary for God.

Spend some time in prayer, asking God for what He would have you do. Then go forward and do it, knowing that God is with you every step of the way.

My Savior and King, You have placed me in this particular time,
among these particular people, for a particular purpose. So I
come before You, asking what You would have me do. Where
would You have me walk as I go forward into this day with You?

ULTIMATE ACCEPTANCE

His wife said to him...."Curse God and die."

JOB 2:9 NLT

We all have people in our lives who, when trouble comes, want to see us turn our backs on God and His Word. After all, doing so probably makes sense to them, so why not to us, right? Wrong. We know better. Just like Job, we can respond, "Should we accept only good things from the hand of God and never anything bad?" (verse 10 NLT). So, when times get tough, when it looks like all has been lost, when others are anxious for you to "curse God and die," keep your faith and keep your eyes on God, knowing that with and in Him alone are your hope and future.

My heart is focused, and my eyes are on You, Lord. Although trouble may come into my life, I will neither fear nor despair. For in You alone are my hope and future, my life and light.

THE POWER OF FOCUS

"What I always feared has happened to me.
What I dreaded has come true. I have no peace,
no quietness. I have no rest; only trouble comes."
JOB 3:25–26 NLT

What we focus on we give power to. If our minds, hearts, and souls are concentrating on the peace of Jesus, we shall have peace. Constantly worrying about "what-ifs" will drive us from God's pathway. That's why the writers of the New Testament would have us think of good things, things that are lovely and praise-worthy. So, if you find your mind driving into the ditch, pick up your Bible and find some uplifting verses to get you back on God's highway. In so doing, you will discover His peace, revel in quietness, and luxuriate in rest.

Lord, what-if scenarios are careening around in
my mind, so much so that I cannot stand. So I come
to You, seeking a good word to get me back on my
feet. Enlighten my mind with a scripture passage
that will lift my heart and draw me closer to You.

A MIDNIGHT MANTRA

In peace I will both lie down and sleep, for You, Lord,
alone make me dwell in safety and confident trust.

PSALM 4:8 AMPC

If you ever have trouble sleeping, memorize the words to this verse and make it a midnight mantra. Commit to saying it in your mind at least ten times, and chances are, you'll fall asleep before hitting number six. Why? Because this is a truth that cannot be denied. In God, nothing at all can harm us. So there's no need to bother yourself with worries. No need to sleep with one eye (and both ears) open. Simply allow yourself to relax, imagining God is like the mattress that is supporting you, that holds you up. Close your eyes and go to sleep, knowing you can do so because God never does (see Psalm 121:4).

As I lay my body down to rest, I imagine You supporting me as I seek the peace and comfort I crave. Ease my mind, emptying it of all worries and fears. Stay awake beside me, sheltering me from storms, encompassing me in Your arms as I settle into sleep.

HOME SAFE

GOD's a safe-house for the battered, a sanctuary
during bad times. The moment you arrive, you
relax; you're never sorry you knocked.
PSALM 9:9–10 MSG

In this world, Jesus said, we'll encounter some trouble. But thank God for God! When we are being pursued, when we need shelter, when we feel as if we are running for our lives, we can go to Him. He will always be there for us—we merely need to remind ourselves of His presence. And, amazingly enough, as soon as we arrive on His doorstep, we know we are home safe. With Him, nothing can harm us. Back in His safe house, we breathe a sigh of relief, then find ourselves smiling, shaking our heads, wondering why in the world it took us so long to get ourselves there and asking ourselves why we left in the first place.

I'm running to You, Lord, knowing You are always there for
me with Your arms open wide. You are my shelter, my safe
house, a place where I am always welcome and can find
the peace my heart, mind, body, soul, and spirit crave.

DIRECT ACCESS

In my distress [when seemingly closed in] I called
upon the Lord and cried to my God; He heard my
voice out of His temple (heavenly dwelling place),
and my cry came before Him, into His [very] ears.
PSALM 18:6 AMPC

Our Lord is so many things. Our Rock, Refuge, Shield, Deliverer, Strength, Hiding Place. . . The list goes on and on. No matter what our situation, no matter what our agony, no matter how hemmed in we feel on every side, we can call out to our Lord and He will hear us. There's no call waiting. We have direct access. And as soon as He hears our cry, He begins reaching out His arms to lift us out of the muddy pit or deep waters we've gotten ourselves into. Oh what a Savior!

I call to You, Lord. Hear my voice, respond with love, and pull me up out of the deep waters. I lift my arms to meet with Yours. As I rise up out of the muck and mire, Your calm replaces my chaos.

AN ENLIGHTENED WAY

You light a lamp for me. The LORD, my God, lights
up my darkness. In your strength I can crush an
army; with my God I can scale any wall.
PSALM 18:28–29 NLT

When we feel all is lost, we may, at first, turn somewhat reluctantly to the Word. After all, solely focused on our troubles, we barely have the energy to reach out for God's help and guidance. But we do so anyway because God's Spirit within compels us. The Holy Spirit knows that not only will the light of God's Word reveal our situation for what it truly is—temporary—but it will give us the strength, strategy, power, and light to overcome any darkness.

When I find myself lost in the wilderness, may Your Spirit
come to my rescue and give me the light to find Your Word.
Give me a new perspective, Lord, so I can see my situation
for what it truly is—temporary. Bless me with the strength
and power to overcome any remaining darkness.

NO LACK

The Lord is my Shepherd [to feed,
guide, and shield me], I shall not lack.
PSALM 23:1 AMPC

God gives us food, guidance, protection. He leads us to a place where we can refresh and restore our souls and spirits. We need not fear, for He has His rod to defend us and His staff to steer us. And if we, for some reason, should veer off the path, chances are He'll leave the other ninety-nine and come after us. What love and commitment!

Each day, take the time to envision following the Lord to lovely pastures. In His presence, lie down and listen to the trickle of a stream before you. Know that the Lord your Shepherd is all you need. Because of Him, you shall not lack.

Because of You, Lord, I lack nothing. Lead me to Your sweet
green pastures. As I lie down in Your presence, I hear the
stream of clear water wending its way beside me. In You
I find my peace, my rest, my place, and my refuge.

GOD'S GOODNESS

I would have lost heart, unless I had believed that I
would see the goodness of the LORD in the land of the
living. Wait on the LORD; be of good courage, and He
shall strengthen your heart; wait, I say, on the LORD!
PSALM 27:13–14 NKJV

There are times when we are so low it's almost hard to breathe, so grieved that we cannot see beyond the shadows. It is then that we need to take the words of Psalm 27:13–14 to heart. Know, live, and breathe the fact that you *will* once again see God's goodness just where you stand, in this land of the living. He *will* lift you up, shine His light, reveal His wonders. It may not happen overnight— but it *will* happen! So take heart. Be brave. Wait for God to work His magic. For He undoubtedly will.

I take a deep breath in this moment, finding calm in
the knowledge that I will see Your goodness in this,
the land of the living. You will lift me up, Lord, shine
Your light, and reveal Your blessing. In You I will find
the strength and courage to await Your wonders.

NEW DIRECTION

You are my hiding place; you protect me from trouble.
You surround me with songs of victory. . . . The LORD
says, "I will guide you along the best pathway for
your life. I will advise you and watch over you."
PSALM 32:7–8 NLT

On those days when we feel we cannot face the world, we have a place to hide—in God. He is our refuge *and* our outer, impenetrable shield. He will build us up and, before we know it, we will be coming out from our hiding place, smiling and singing, knowing God has given us the victory. From that point forward, a new road map is made. He gives us new direction, showing us the best way to go, all the while keeping His eyes on us, making sure we come to no harm.

My soul yearns to hide in You today, Lord. There I pray You'd protect me from trouble, surround me with Your impenetrable shield, and restore my spirit. When I am rested, give me the courage to embark upon a new path with You by my side.

WORD POWER

The LORD merely spoke, and the heavens were created.
He breathed the word, and all the stars were born.
PSALM 33:6 NLT

What power our God has. He says just a few words, and the sky is born. He simply breathes, and all the stars and planets suddenly pop into existence. And the wonder of all this is that He is still speaking His Word into each person's life today. He is constantly creating new and breathtaking things. What's even more awesome is that we have access to His powerful, all-creating words. They can be found in the Bible. Today, speak one of God's promises into your life. Believe it is true. Then stand back and watch it manifest itself—another one of God's wonders before your very eyes.

Speak Your Word into my life today, Lord. Lead me to the promise You would have me lean into. Help me speak it into my own life, to accept it as fact. Then give me the patience to stand back and watch Your promise manifest itself before my very eyes.

SOLELY DIFFERENT

*The LORD looks from heaven; he sees all the sons
of men.... He fashions their hearts individually.*
PSALM 33:13, 15 NKJV

There are all kinds of different people in this world, from the swirl
on the top of their head to the footprints they leave behind. So it's
no wonder we may chance across people who rub us the wrong
way—and vice versa. Yet our Maker knows we are all different,
each having a special talent to share or role to play. So if someone is getting on your nerves, stop and consider how, although
different, we all are the same in one respect: we are here to love
one another and God. Then praise Him for fashioning each of our
hearts individually. And ask Him for the strength to respond to
all with His love.

*Lord, when I'm frustrated with the people around me,
remind me that each person You've created is precious.
Everyone has a purpose in this life, a gift to share,
a role to play. Then, Lord, give me the strength to
respond in love to every person I encounter.*

HEARTILY WHOLE

Our inner selves wait [earnestly] for the Lord; He is our Help
and our Shield. For in Him does our heart rejoice, because we
have trusted (relied on and been confident) in His holy name.
PSALM 33:20–21 AMPC

We all have a God-shaped hole in us, an inner yearning to connect with our Creator. And when in prayer we feel ourselves united with Him on a deep spiritual level, we cannot help but smile. For His presence cannot help but fill our hearts with joy and light.

Having trouble making that connection? Then do a heart check. Are you relying on Him—and only Him—for everything, with complete trust and total certainty? If not, surrender all to Him today, then ask and allow Him to make you heartily whole.

Help me, Lord, to take myself off the throne of my
heart and put You there instead. Help me to rely on
You alone for everything. Remind me each day to
surrender all I am, have, and hope to be to You.

ALREADY THERE

*GOD met me more than halfway, he freed me from
my anxious fears. . . . GOD's angel sets up a circle of
protection around us while we pray. . . . Young lions on
the prowl get hungry, but GOD-seekers are full of God.*

PSALM 34:4, 7, 10 MSG

When you can barely cry out because you are muted with fear, God
rushes over. He is instantly by your side, unlocking the chains of
anxiety and trepidation holding you captive. From the first word
of your prayer to the last, His angels are clamoring in, protecting
you on every side. Within that circle, nothing can touch, harm,
or disturb you. Because you have sought God, He has taken up
residence within you, filling you with His joy and presence. Lean
back on God today. Imagine His angels surrounding you. Revel in
the fullness of God-given freedom.

---

*In this moment, I seek Your face, Lord. I long to come into Your
presence. Welcome me there! Then send Your angels to create
a circle of protection around me. Fill me with Your light and
life as I revel in the freedom with which You have blessed me!*

EVEN DEEPER

The Lord is near to the brokenhearted and saves those who are crushed in spirit. Many are the afflictions of the righteous, but the Lord delivers him out of them all.

PSALM 34:18–19 NASB

There is something comforting knowing that God is right there when your heart is aching or broken, when your spirit seems totally crushed—by the death of a loved one, a divorce, the loss of a very much needed job, or a terminal illness. When you are at your lowest, take solace in the fact that God is by your side, wiping away each of your tears with His gentle hand and drawing you even deeper into Himself and His embrace. Allow deep to call to deep, knowing you will yet praise Him.

When I am filled with sorrow, I take comfort in the truth that You, Lord, are by my side. I pray You would wipe the tears from my face. Draw me deeper into Your embrace. Envelop my spirit with Yours. Remind me that this sorrow will pass.

DREAMS AND DESIRES

*Delight yourself also in the Lord, and He will give you the desires
and secret petitions of your heart. Commit your way to the Lord
[roll and repose each care of your load on Him]; trust (lean on,
rely on, and be confident) also in Him and He will bring it to pass.*
PSALM 37:4–5 AMPC

When you get yourself into God, finding the joy of being with Him
more valuable than anything else in life, He can't help but make
your secret heartfelt desires come true. As you commit all that you
are to Him, putting each and every worry and fear onto His much
stronger and broader shoulders, fully trusting He will make all
come out right, He'll turn your dreams into reality—regardless of
whether you are nine, forty-nine, or ninety-nine. You can depend
upon it—and Him.

*I commit myself entirely to You, Lord. For You are the
dream maker, the one who transforms hopes into reality.
To You I give all my cares. In You I trust, and on You I rely,
knowing You will one day bring my desires to fruition.*

THE ULTIMATE SUPPORT

The steps of a [good] man are directed and established by the Lord when He delights in his way [and He busies Himself with his every step]. Though he falls, he shall not be utterly cast down, for the Lord grasps his hand in support and upholds him.

PSALM 37:23–24 AMPC

The bad news is we may go through some rough patches in this life. The good news is we won't be going through them alone—nor for very long. When we follow the path God lays out for us, we find Him on every corner. Delighted in our direction, He focuses on each step we take. And as soon as He sees us stumble, He reaches out, grabs our hand, and gets us back on our feet. Walking God's way, we have all the support we need to bear up under anything—and everything!

I tripped up, Lord. Yet I thank You for not allowing me to fall flat on my face. Help me get back up on my feet, Lord. Steady me during this rough patch in my life. Open my eyes so that I will see Your clear direction.

ALL IN ONE

He drew me up out of a horrible pit [a pit of tumult and of destruction], out of the miry clay (froth and slime), and set my feet upon a rock, steadying my steps and establishing my goings.

PSALM 40:2 AMPC

Not only does God lift you up out of the deepest abyss, out of the ooze in which you'd almost sunk, He sets your feet high upon a rock to keep you secure and close to Him. He holds on to you until you are steady. He teaches you how to walk again and helps to put you back on the right path. All in one verse, God proves to be your rescuer, protector, and guide. It doesn't get much better than that!

I thank You, Lord, for pulling me up out of the pit into which I'd sunk—for getting me back on my feet. Now I ask that You help to steady my feet and guide me back upon the right path.

GETTING AWAY

*Let be and be still, and know (recognize
and understand) that I am God.*

PSALM 46:10 AMPC

It's time to stop running around. Get away from all the distractions, everything that is vying for your attention. Stop, stand, sit where you are. Simply be still. Don't just do something, stand there! Take three deep breaths and revel in the stillness that is part of God's perfect peace. To any issues that come up in your mind, respond with "So what. . . . God is taking care of all." In other words, let all things be. In this stillness of body and mind, rest in, know of, and seek God's face. He's waiting. Allow your soul to fly away from the world and meet Him where He is, spirit to Spirit.

---

*Lord, I admit that I may have gotten distracted. So I come and
bow at Your feet, asking that You would give me the calm I need
to be still in Your presence. To let what is, be. To remember
I don't need to worry because You are handling it all.*

THAT SECRET PLACE

*He who dwells in the secret place of the Most High shall
remain stable and fixed under the shadow of the Almighty
[Whose power no foe can withstand]. I will say of the
Lord, He is my Refuge and my Fortress, my God; on Him
I lean and rely, and in Him I [confidently] trust!*
PSALM 91:1–2 AMPC

Constantly living in communion with God, nothing can disturb
your peace of mind. Steadily abiding with and in Him, there is a
peace beyond understanding, for you know that God can vanquish
anything and everything—fear, hatred, grief, sorrow. Such a life is
a testimony to others of your living faith and the strength, protection, and power of your God. And it all begins in that secret place
where you can "take refuge and be confident until calamities and
destructive storms are passed" (Psalm 57:1 AMPC).

---

*I know, Lord, that all things are in Your hands. You can,
do, and will vanquish all the darkness that touches my life.
And so, in You I take refuge, confident I will be protected
until the storm clouds and shadows have passed.*

ONE HEARTFELT VERSE

I will meditate on Your precepts, and contemplate Your ways.
I will delight myself in Your statutes; I will not forget Your word.
PSALM 119:15–16 NKJV

It's one thing to read God's Word. It's another to meditate upon it, really taking time to soak in it, allowing it to cover you from head to toe with meaning and deliberation. Then to take the Lord's truth and memorize it, hiding it in your heart so that it becomes part of your life, ready and able to lift you, help you, shield you, free you, guide you. What's one heartfelt verse you can hide in your heart today, one that in all likelihood will save you tomorrow? Think about it. Revel in it. Memorize it. Own it. Live it. And stand amazed at God and His Word-power.

Lord, as I open Your Word, lead me to the verse You would have me own today. Help me memorize it, to hide it in my heart so that Your truth will be close at hand to lift me, help me, guide me, shield me, and save me.

LOOKING FOR HELP

GOD guards you from every evil, he guards your very
life. He guards you when you leave and when you
return, he guards you now, he guards you always.
PSALM 121:7–8 MSG

Where do you look for help and strength? To Mother Nature?
To other people? To money? How about turning to the God who
created everything, the one who breathed each of us into being.
He will never let you stumble. He is awake while you sleep. He is
your guardian, always at your side, keeping you safe from things
visible and invisible. It was true yesterday. It's true today. It will
be true tomorrow. Need or want anything? Look to God. Seek His
face. And, as you go out and as you come in, you will be safe, in
heaven and on earth.

To You alone I look for my help and strength. Guard me
from all things visible and invisible, Lord. Be with me
as I go out and then come in. Watch over me as I sleep,
Lord, cradled in Your presence. Keep me safe always.

A SECOND OPINION

Search me, O God, and know my heart; test me and know
my anxious thoughts. Point out anything in me that
offends you, and lead me along the path of everlasting life.

PSALM 139:23–24 NLT

We think we know what our shortcomings are, the things we need to work on. But sometimes we need a second opinion. That's where God comes in. Only He, it seems, can reveal what is truly in our hearts and minds. After all, our holiness is an inside job—and God's just the person to do it. It is He who will help us discover what is not in line with Him and what we can do to change things up. Once we've had a good examination from the Great Physician, the right remedy is not far behind.

Reveal to me, Lord, what is truly in my heart and mind.
Help me discover what is not pleasing in Your eyes.
Show me what I can do to be more aligned with
You, my Lord and Master, my heart and life.

MOUTH GUARD

Set a guard, O LORD, over my mouth;
keep watch over the door of my lips.
PSALM 141:3 NKJV

How easily things seem to slip out of our mouths. In the heat of an argument, irretrievable words tumble out. In our distractedness, thoughtless phrases pass our lips and we are unaware of their effect on others. So what are you, a woman of the way, to do? Ask God to place a holy sentry, a guard over your mouth—not so much to shield your teeth but to protect others from potentially painful criticism, cutting insults, and angry barbs. Instead of such discourse, take the right course: go with compliments instead of criticism, insights instead of insults, blessings instead of barbs. Speak with love, and witness the healing power of your words.

Sometimes, Lord, I say things I shouldn't. And the next thing I know, I have hurt another person, which means I have hurt You—and perhaps even myself. So I ask You, Lord, to help me speak to everyone—including myself—with love and words of healing.

WAKE-UP CALL

Cause me to hear Your loving-kindness in the morning,
for on You do I lean and in You do I trust. Cause me to know
the way wherein I should walk, for I lift up my inner self to You.
PSALM 143:8 AMPC

What a joy to wake up in the morning, hearing the sound of God's adoring voice. What an awesome start to anyone's day. And how about returning the greeting by raising your arms to the heavens, exclaiming, "Good morning, God! What are we going to do today?" By exhibiting your trust in Him at the break of day, you'll be setting up the pattern for the hours to come, until night falls, and your heart, mind, body, and soul are again cradled in His arms.

Oh Lord, what sweetness I find when I seek and listen to Your
voice in the morning hours. Thank You for always being with
me in each new day. Now, what are we going to do today?

THE RIGHT PATH

*Trust in the Lord with all your heart and do not lean on your
own understanding. In all your ways acknowledge Him,
and He will make your paths straight.*

God is all-knowing, all-seeing, all-present. That's why you can trust
Him to make the right decisions, to head you in the right direction. It doesn't matter if what He wants you to do seems illogical
or incomprehensible. God can see everything everywhere—past,
present, and future. But we mere earthbound mortals have
extremely limited vision. So trust that God will always know better
than you, your friends, and your relatives. Put all your faith in
Him, follow His directions, and you will always be on the right
path—His.

---

*Help me, Lord, to trust that You know better than anyone
what direction I should go today, what decision I should
make. Knowing You can see what lies ahead, I put all my
faith in You, for You will lead me down the right path.*

HEART WISE

Guard your heart above all else,
for it determines the course of your life.

PROVERBS 4:23 NLT

King Solomon, a supposedly wise man, did not watch his heart very carefully. During his reign over Israel, he fell in love with many foreign women and ended up following their gods. In fact, 1 Kings 11:4 (NKJV) says that "his wives turned his heart after other gods; and his heart was not loyal to the LORD his God." As a result of his split loyalty, the country of Israel divided after his death. So heed diligently Proverbs 4:23. Keep a sharp eye on where your heart's desires may be leading you, and above all else, make sure it's not away from but toward God, the pilot of your life.

Lord, Your Word tells me that, above all else, I should
guard my heart—not allow it to lead me astray. So help
me keep a sharp eye on where my desires are leading
me. I seek Your will and way above all other things.

EXPOSÉ ON THOUGHTS

For as he [a man] thinks in his heart, so is he.
PROVERBS 23:7 AMPC

It's amazing how many things we won't put down the garbage disposal because we know what will clog, injure, or fatally wound it. Yet we are not, perhaps, so vigilant with what we put in our own heads. The phrase "You are what you eat" could equally apply to thoughts: "You are what you think." If you expose your mind to nothing but dire, discouraging, and destructive information, you're bound to be a negative person. If you expose your mind to hopeful, encouraging, and affirming information, you're going to be a positive person. So keep your mind on praiseworthy things. When you do, you'll be so much more apt to worship than worry. What do you think?

Oh Lord, heaven only knows what garbage is clogging up my mind and heart. So I ask You, Lord, to help me expose myself to helpful and hopeful information. To keep my mind on my blessings not curses. To seek good not evil. To worship rather than worry.

THE TRUTH OF GOD'S MATTER

The believer replied, "Every promise of God proves true;
he protects everyone who runs to him for help.
So don't second-guess him; he might take
you to task and show up your lies."

PROVERBS 30:5–6 MSG

God's Word is truth. Every promise He makes will be upheld. Knowing He will never forsake us and never let us go is the mental armor we wear and spiritual weapon we bear as we go forth into this world. Along with this confidence, we must be content with what God has chosen to reveal to humankind in His Word. Thus, we are not to add to it, for He has already laid out in the Bible all we need to know. Endeavor only to rest and trust in God and the Word He has gifted us—both amazing treasures beyond compare.

I'm running to You for help, Lord. I may be out of breath,
but I am not out of faith. So I ask You, Lord, to help me
trust in You and Your Word. May I put more assurance
in Your promises than in my problems or property.

A NATURALLY
VIRTUOUS WOMAN

A good woman is hard to find,
and worth far more than diamonds.
PROVERBS 31:10 MSG

The woman described in Proverbs 31:10–31 is enough to make anyone wonder how she could ever become such a strong woman, or even come close! Yet it obviously can be done. How? By being a woman of strong faith and spirit. If a woman's heart, mind, body, and soul are dedicated to and worshipful of God, all the other virtues of Proverbs 31—willing to work, constructive, wise, gracious, generous, fearless, encouraging, financially prudent, dignified, watchful—will come naturally to her. Charm and beauty are nice but are not needed by a virtuous woman who spends more time reflecting upon God than her own image in the makeup mirror.

Help me, Lord, to become the woman You created me to be. Remind me that, although it's nice to be charming and pretty, it's better to be a woman after Your own heart. Make me a woman of strong faith and spirit, worshipping You instead of my bank account or complexion.

CHANGE

There is an appointed time for everything.
And there is a time for every event under heaven.
ECCLESIASTES 3:1 NASB

We go through many transitions in life. Some of those are brought about by God—the seasons, birth and death, sowing and reaping. Others are brought about by our own choices—crying and laughing, holding on and letting go, breaking down and building up. We witness the waxing and waning of things in our own bodies as we grow from girl into woman and beyond. Instead of resisting these inevitable changes, those within and outside of our control, may we revel in the present and praise God for each transition that draws us closer and closer to Him, our rock and our refuge, the one who never changes.

Time seems so fleeting, Lord. Yet You are eternal. And someday I will be with You forever and always. So help me relax in the present, Lord, and not get hung up on things beyond my control. I desire complete rest in You, my rock and refuge.

THE POWER OF LOVE

Love is as strong as death, its jealousy as enduring as the
grave. Love flashes like fire, the brightest kind of flame.
Many waters cannot quench love, nor can rivers drown it.
SONG OF SOLOMON 8:6–7 NLT

Love is the greatest force in the universe, for love is God. And
nothing—not even the greatest rivers and oceans—can separate us from or overpower that love. What an amazing force, our
love for God and His love for us. It cannot even be overcome by
death, as Christ proved when He rose again. And how wonderful to
know that we have the power to extend this love not only to God
but to each other. Who can you empower with your love today?

You, Lord, are love. And nothing can separate me
from You. No matter what happens, You are my
eternal source of love and light. Show me, Lord. . . .
Who would You have me empower with Your love today?

PERFECT PEACE

You will guard him and keep him in perfect and constant
peace whose mind [both its inclination and its character]
is stayed on You, because he commits himself to You,
leans on You, and hopes confidently in You.
ISAIAH 26:3 AMPC

When your focus is on God and stays there, you will experience
heavenly peace. And not just peace with and in God, but with other
people, circumstances, yourself, the past, and the future. This
inward, outward, backward, forward peace is what you find yourself
tending to seek more and more as you realize that nothing else in
this world but complete dependence, trust, and hope in God can
give you the serenity you long for. With God guarding the door to
your mind, how can you *not* have peace?

Lord, I long for the peace only You can provide.
So I commit everything I have, all that I am
and hope to be, to You. Stay close, Lord.

ASKING FOR DIRECTIONS

Your ears shall hear a word behind you, saying,
"This is the way, walk in it," whenever you turn to
the right hand or whenever you turn to the left.

ISAIAH 30:21 NKJV

Whenever we ask God for help, He immediately responds. The problem is that too often, instead of calling out to God, we try to make choices or decisions based on our own knowledge, experience, or hunches. Even worse is when we ask the advice of anyone and everyone *but* God! Yet God has told us that He is more than willing to direct us—and *He's* the one who truly knows what's best for us. So, got a decision to make? Stop. Ask God for guidance. Listen for His answer. And then, and only then, move forward.

Lord, I'm tired of making decisions on my own based on
nothing but hunches and human knowledge. So I reach
out to You for guidance. I open my ears to Your voice.
Tell me which path to take. Direct where You would
have me go. I won't take another step until You do!

SIMPLY REMEMBER

*Have you not known? Have you not heard? The everlasting
God, the LORD, the Creator of the ends of the earth, neither
faints nor is weary. His understanding is unsearchable.*

ISAIAH 40:28 NKJV

We *do* know and we *have* heard it before. But sometimes we apparently need a reminder that God is humongous, inexhaustible, wise beyond measure, constantly vigilant, and forever compassionate. There is nothing that will surprise Him. There is nothing we have not done or will do that He won't forgive. Remember the infinite one? He sees everything and everyone. He's more powerful than any foe. And He's got your back. So relax. Simply remember: There is no one and no*thing* like our mighty God!

---

*Thank You, Lord, for the compassion and love You continually
show me and for the strength and energy You continually
provide me. Help me stay calm, knowing You always have my
back. Remind me every moment of the day that I don't need
to fear anything or anyone because You are by my side.*

THE MASTER

He gives power to the weak, and to those
who have no might He increases strength.

ISAIAH 40:29 NKJV

We want to be involved in lots of things—to help at church, school, the community, and our own family. But when we do it all in our own energy, we're bound to run out of oomph at some point. So when you do find yourself weakening or completely out of strength, call on God. He'll power you right back up—and may even give you guidance as to what activities to continue and which ones to forgo for now. Because, although it's wonderful to be of service to others, your main obligation is hanging out with the Master.

I may have too many things on my plate, Lord.
Would You please help me figure out which activities I
should continue and which I should forgo for now? I never
want to be too busy for You—the one who powers me up.

LIKE EAGLES

*But those who wait for the Lord [who expect, look for,
and hope in Him] shall change and renew their strength
and power; they shall lift their wings and mount up [close to
God] as eagles [mount up to the sun]; they shall run and not
be weary, they shall walk and not faint or become tired.*

ISAIAH 40:31 AMPC

It's awe-inspiring when we watch eagles flying high above the earth.
How they soar on those wings! It's such an elegant demonstration
of their power and strength. We, who don't just tap our toes while
waiting for the Lord, are like those eagles. We "expect, look for,
and hope" in God, knowing that He will renew us, recharge us, the
closer we get to Him. Keep this in mind as you take flight today.

---

*My eagle eyes are on You, Lord, as I mount up on the wings
of my faith. I am filled with hope and great expectations
for what You will do in my life. Renew my strength and
power so I can soar into the heavens and into Your
presence. What's our flight plan today, Lord?*

REMEMBER GOD

"Don't be afraid, for I am with you. Don't be discouraged,
for I am your God. I will strengthen you and help you.
I will hold you up with my victorious right hand."
ISAIAH 41:10 NLT

How awesome not to be afraid, to have our strength so tied up with God that we come out of nail-biting situations victorious! And that's what this verse promises us. So no matter what you might be up against, how scary a situation may seem, how dark the future looks, remember God. Remember who you are in Him. Consider how much He's done for you already. Take strength from His Word. And walk on, knowing that in Him you have all the victories you need.

Knowing You are with me gives me hope and strength. Stay close today, Lord. Power me up with Your Word. Remind me that, in You, I—a woman of Your Way—will find victory.

DIRECT COURAGE

This is what the LORD says—he who created you,
Jacob, he who formed you, Israel: "Do not fear."
ISAIAH 43:1 NIV

In His Word, God keeps telling us not to be afraid. In fact, there are at least 365 do-not-be-afraid-type phrases in the Bible—one for each day of the year. That must mean God really wants us to get it through our heads, know it in our hearts, declare it in our minds, and confirm it in our souls. God, who intricately formed you, knows exactly what you are afraid of. So, wise up and listen up. He's telling you directly not to let your particular fears overcome you. How cool is that?

Sometimes, Lord, my fears get the best of me. Yet Your Word
continually tells me not to be afraid. Because I have the
Creator of the universe, the one who called light into being,
in my corner, I never need to—and will not—fear anything!

LIGHTEN UP

"I have called you by name; you are mine. When you go through deep waters, I will be with you. When you go through rivers of difficulty, you will not drown. When you walk through the fire of oppression, you will not be burned up; the flames will not consume you. For I am the LORD, your God."

ISAIAH 43:1–3 NLT

Each one of us wants to matter, to be known and loved by someone—someone who will never leave us, no matter how bad things get. And each of us has that "someone" in God. He has called you by name! He's known you forever! You are His royal daughter. No matter what happens—or where or when—He is with you. So lighten up! You never have been and never will be alone.

Lord, thank You for calling me by name, for knowing me inside and out, and still loving me. Thank You for sticking with me no matter how bad things get and for walking with me on this side of heaven—and the next. Because You're with me, I'll never be alone!

CHANGE UP

"Forget the former things; do not dwell on the past. See, I am doing a new thing! Now it springs up; do you not perceive it? I am making a way in the wilderness and streams in the wasteland."
ISAIAH 43:18–19 NIV

God is constantly changing things up. But people who are stuck in the past or freaked out about the future can miss these new things coming up right now. Such women are letting the past and the future suck out the energy from and blur the vision of what He is creating today! So take a good look around you. Where is God working in your part of the world today? What new thing is He waiting for you to see and take up? Seek—and you'll find it. Move out—and He'll pave your way.

Help me stop living in the past, Lord, and being afraid of what the future may bring. Help me focus on what You are doing in my life today and where You are calling me to go, trusting You will pave the way before me.

GOD'S BABY GIRL

Even to your old age I am He, and even to hair
white with age will I carry you. I have made, and I
will bear; yes, I will carry and will save you.
ISAIAH 46:4 AMPC

Holding a precious baby is one of the most wonderful experiences you can have in this life. You find yourself simply marveling at her ten tiny toes and ten tiny fingers and awestruck at her look of complete dependence upon you. That must be how God feels when He carries you. No matter how old you are, you will always be His baby girl and, whether your hair is that of a newborn or an old woman, you will never be—and never have been—out of His arms.

I can't help but smile imagining You carrying me all through
my life, Lord. I have been in Your arms from the very
beginning and will remain cuddled up against You even after
I depart from this earth! Oh, what comfort this brings!

FATHER KNOWS BEST

"I am the LORD your God, who teaches you what is best
for you, who directs you in the way you should go.
If only you had paid attention to my commands,
your peace would have been like a river,
your well-being like the waves of the sea."
ISAIAH 48:17–18 NIV

How many times have we made a decision without first consulting God and then ended up facing a lot of trouble and heartache? If we had not only listened but obeyed His words, we would have been filled with immense peace and well-being. So the next time a decision comes up, go to God first. Pay attention to Him. Find direction in prayer and in His Word. Then, and only then, move forward in His way, confident that God the Father knows best.

Lord, things never seem to work out when I make decisions
on my own without consulting You first. So I pray, Lord,
that You would help me keep my eyes open to Your presence,
my mind open to Your Word, and my heart open to Your way.

THE MASTERMIND

Seek the LORD while you can find him. Call on him now while he is near.... "My thoughts are nothing like your thoughts," says the LORD. "And my ways are far beyond anything you could imagine."
ISAIAH 55:6, 8 NLT

Why do we want to seek God and call on Him? Because He is *the* mastermind. He is the ultimate in wisdom. He thinks of things we'd never dreamed or imagined and, hence, never even considered! With Him there are no limits! There is no box to think outside of! So, if you've got some choices to make, things to consider, run to God. Seek Him out. Call His name. Ask His advice. He'll blow your human mind!

Here I am, Lord, standing before You. I am eager to seek Your face, take in Your wisdom, and understand Your dream for my life. Speak to me, Lord. Tell me what You would have me do. Blow my mind with the voice of Your Spirit!

FRUITFUL WORDS

*"So is my word that goes out from my mouth: It will
not return to me empty, but will accomplish what I
desire and achieve the purpose for which I sent it."*

ISAIAH 55:11 NIV

God's Word bears amazing fruit. Once it is tasted, it roots itself
in our minds and cannot be shaken loose. It then begins to bear
fruit in our own minds and lives. Anyone who reads or hears the
Word is changed. All that the Word provides—promises, maxims,
proverbs, enlightenment, predictions, guidance—achieves God's
particular purpose. Where are you sowing the seed of God's Word
today? Because of you and His Word, what fruit will God be har-
vesting tomorrow?

---

*God, lead me through Your Word today. Impart to my mind what
verses, wisdom, light, guidance, and promises You would like
me to plant in my heart and allow to take root. Then work Your
power upon me, helping that seed to bear good fruit for You.*

HOPE-FILLED PROMISE

"I'll show up and take care of you as I promised. . . . I know what I'm doing. I have it all planned out—plans to take care of you, not abandon you, plans to give you the future you hope for."
JEREMIAH 29:10–11 MSG

Some days things just don't seem to go right. We wonder if we're on the right track, doing what God created us to do. Or are we walking down a path He never wanted us on in the first place? Not to worry. If you are headed the wrong way, God will show up, cut you off at the pass, and turn you in the right direction. He knows what He's doing. He's got it all planned out for you. Your future is safe in His hands. That's His promise.

Lord, give me confidence that You are watching over me. That You are taking care of me. That You have my life all planned out. That I'm doing what You created me to do. I know my past, present, and future are safe in Your hands!

GOD'S PERSPECTIVE

*"I am the LORD, the God of all the peoples
of the world. Is anything too hard for me?"*
JEREMIAH 32:27 NLT

The above verse is similar to what God said to Abraham and Sarah after she laughed at the idea of becoming pregnant in her old age (see Genesis 18:14). Two other times, God asked people if they thought His *arm* was too short to accomplish things (see Numbers 11:23 and Isaiah 59:1). But Jesus put a different twist on these verses, saying, "What is impossible for people is possible with God" (Luke 18:27 NLT). Looking at things from our limited perspective, we see impossibilities. But when seeing things from God's promised perspective, suddenly a myriad of solutions abound. Got a problem? Go get God. He's got the answers you need.

---

*Lord, I need some answers. You, God of all people,
have unlimited perspective and power. Help me to remember
that what seems impossible to me is more than possible for You!*

SOURCE OF KNOWLEDGE

Call to Me and I will answer you and show you great and mighty things, fenced in and hidden, which you do not know (do not distinguish and recognize, have knowledge of and understand).

JEREMIAH 33:3 AMPC

It's humbling trying to imagine all the things we don't know. Fortunately, we have God, who knows it all. He sees things that have been hidden for eons. And He is thoroughly familiar with everything—in heaven and on earth, visible and invisible. But how do we access this far-reaching knowledge? Through prayer, meditation, and reading God's Word. Just pose God a question, ask for an answer, and keep your eyes and ears open. He'll show you what you need to know.

Here I am, Lord, calling upon You again. I need Your help and guidance. Lead me to what You would have me know as I read Your Word, meditate upon it, then pray in Your presence. I will ask my questions and then patiently await Your answers.

STUCK ON EACH OTHER

*There's one other thing I remember, and remembering,
I keep a grip on hope: GOD's loyal love couldn't have run
out, his merciful love couldn't have dried up. They're
created new every morning. How great your faithfulness!
I'm sticking with GOD (I say it over and over).*

LAMENTATIONS 3:21–24 MSG

Our God is a God of abundance. His love and mercy for us have no end. They are newly made every morning. How wonderful, this endless supply of second, third, fourth, fifth chances for us. No matter how much we've messed things up by our words or acts, God will still love us and still have mercy on us. He's so stuck on us, we can't help but be stuck on Him.

Thank You, Lord, for Your unending love and mercy. Your fresh love awaits me—it greets me every morning. Your mercy is there for me, no matter how many times I may stumble. In You alone, I hope. On You alone, I rely. Shower me with Your love!

THE SEEKING WOMAN

GOD proves to be good to the man who passionately waits,
to the woman who diligently seeks. . . . When life is heavy
and hard to take, go off by yourself. Enter the silence.
Bow in prayer. Don't ask questions: wait for hope to appear.
LAMENTATIONS 3:25, 28–29 MSG

What great advice for us on days when we are troubled and weary of life, with no energy left to nurture anyone—including ourselves. Go to God your refuge, whether it be a physical place or a mental one. Walk into the silence and commune with the Master. Don't worry about what to say or ask. God knows what's on your mind. Just expect His answer and His presence, as promised to all women who diligently seek.

I'm running to You in this moment, Lord. I need a minute or
two—or three—alone with You. I fold my hands in prayer,
resting in Your presence. I wait in confidence, knowing Your
hope will give me the strength to rise again in Your name.

TRANSFORMED

*"I'll give you a new heart, put a new spirit in you. I'll remove the
stone heart from your body and replace it with a heart that's
God-willed, not self-willed. I'll put my Spirit in you and make it
possible for you to do what I tell you and live by my commands."*
EZEKIEL 36:26–27 MSG

When you allow Jesus into your heart, everything changes. You
become more gentle, more sensitive to others. You find your priorities, concerns, and dreams are different. It suddenly seems
easier to understand God, and you begin thirsting for His Word.
You are a new creature in Christ. With a brand-new heart and
spirit, you are transformed, ready and eager to make today and
every day all about God, in whom you live, move, and have your
being. Suddenly, anything for God is possible. Remember that as
you step into this day.

---

*Jesus, before this day gets hectic, I come to You, inviting You into
my heart. Help me plan this day according to what You would
have me do, say, and be. Help me to make this day all about You.
I know that with You, anything and everything is possible!*

ALONGSIDE

"I see four men loose, walking in the midst of the fire; and they are not hurt, and the form of the fourth is like the Son of God."
DANIEL 3:25 NKJV

There are times in life when we feel as if we have been forced into a fiery furnace. With no apparent chance of escape, we cry out to God, "Where are You, Lord?" Yet we need not shout. For Jesus, the Son of God, is in that furnace with us. Whatever trial we face, we can be assured that He is walking alongside us. *And* that we will not only come out of this situation, but will do so intact. It's nothing but the best of God for those who trust and serve Him!

Thank You, Jesus, for being with me when I walk through the fire. I open my eyes and heart to Your presence and comfort. With You beside me in any and every trial, I know that I will not only come out intact, but victorious!

A PRAISEWORTHY LESSON

*"When my sanity returned to me, so did my honor
and glory and kingdom.... Now I, Nebuchadnezzar,
praise and glorify and honor the King of heaven. All his
acts are just and true, and he is able to humble the proud."*

DANIEL 4:36–37 NLT

It's amazing what happens when we let pride come between us and God. When Nebuchadnezzar accredited all his greatness to himself and himself alone, God announced the great king would become beastlike—and he did! Then, as predicted, Nebuchadnezzar's sanity returned, and he once again reigned, even greater than before in riches and humility, giving all credit to the Lord God. A praiseworthy lesson for us all.

---

*All I am and hope to be is due to You, Lord. Thank You
for being in my life, for walking with me through the
fire and amid the flood. I give credit for all I have and
am to You. Without You in my life, I am nothing.*

ANGELS WON, LIONS ZERO

Then the king. . .commanded that Daniel should be taken up out of the den. So Daniel was taken up out of the den, and no hurt of any kind was found on him because he believed in (relied on, adhered to, and trusted in) his God.

DANIEL 6:23 AMPC

King Darius passed a law stating no one was to pray to anyone but him. Daniel, knowing full well that this edict was in effect, prayed to his God anyway—and he did so "three times a day, just as he had always done" (Daniel 6:10 NLT)! Because of Daniel's courage and steadfast faith, he survived the lions' den with nary a scratch on him. So be bold and brave in faith today, knowing God's angels will disempower any lions you may face.

Knowing that Your angels surround me with a ring of protection, I can face anything this world throws at me, Lord. Because I believe in and rely on You, I can be bold and brave in faith today and every day!

THE HOLY GRID

What are you waiting for? Return to your God!
Commit yourself in love, in justice! Wait for
your God, and don't give up on him—ever!
HOSEA 12:6 MSG

How many times do we get sidetracked and begin doing things in our own strength, forgetting that God is the ultimate power source? Why do we always seem to wander away from the holy grid? It's time to stop being impatient, running ahead of God, and doing things on our own. Stop. Turn around. Head back to God. Commit to Him, allowing His love to flow through you. Be assured that all good things will come to you, a woman who waits patiently on the Master.

I'll admit, Lord, that sometimes I get involved in earthly
happenings and forget You're beside me. Then I start
lagging behind or running ahead of what You would have
me be and do. So I'm heading back to You, Lord, patiently
waiting for Your direction before I take another step!

DREAMS AND VISIONS

"I will pour out my Spirit on every kind of people:
your sons will prophesy, also your daughters. Your old
men will dream, your young men will see visions. I'll even
pour out my Spirit on the servants, men and women both."
JOEL 2:28–29 MSG

You are a servant of God and a believer in Christ. As such, the Holy Spirit hasn't just been sprinkled on you. He has been *poured out* on you! Your cup runneth over! As you continually obey God, the Spirit empowers you more and more. What dreams and visions is He giving you? Are you living them out? Ask God for clarity and guidance today. Know that you are the Spirit-filled dreamer God envisioned before you were even born.

I'm Your servant, Lord, the daughter on whom You have poured
out Your Spirit. Open my mind and soul to the dreams and visions
You have planned for me since the beginning of time. Help me
to see them clearly and live them out as I walk in Your way.

DO-GOODERS

Seek good and not evil—and live! You talk
about GOD, the God-of-the-Angel-Armies,
being your best friend. Well, live like it. . . . Hate evil
and love good, then work it out in the public square.

AMOS 5:14–15 MSG

To follow Christ is to continually seek to do good. Not just talk about it—but be so filled with love for God and His people, that we can't help but do the right thing! And not just in church on Sundays or on mission trips. But everywhere! Every place on this earth is a mission field for God, for doing the right thing, for being honest, selfless, loving, kind, decent. Humbly take responsibility when due. Remember that doing the good thing is doing the God thing.

Lord, help me to seek good in this world. Help me to
not just talk love but be love. Make me a woman who
does the right thing, the good thing, the honest, selfless,
loving, kind, and decent thing—the God thing.

THE BOOMERANG EFFECT

*As you have done, it shall be done to you; your
dealings will return upon your own head.*
OBADIAH 1:15 AMPC

There's no doubt about it. What we do will come right back at us.
We will reap what we sow, some of it sooner rather than later.
So what are you sowing? Seeds of love, respect, honor, humility,
selflessness? If so, that's what you'll reap further down the road.
So the next time you feel exasperated by fellow humans—the
kids, the husband, the boss, your in-laws, your siblings, your par-
ents, a complete stranger—take a deep breath before you say
or do anything. Ask yourself, "Would I want this boomeranging
back at me?" Then proceed accordingly.

---

*Your spiritual law, the one about reaping what we sow,
is such an important one, Lord. Help me to keep it in mind
as I go through this next minute, hour, day, week, month,
year, life. Train me to treat others like I want to be treated.*

DRY LAND

*"When my soul fainted within me, I remembered
the LORD; and my prayer went up to You,
into Your holy temple."... So the LORD spoke to
the fish, and it vomited Jonah onto dry land.*

JONAH 2:7, 10 NKJV

When we are in too deep, when there seems no way out of the
trouble we've gotten ourselves into, we turn to the Lord. In that
moment of distress and suffocating darkness, we confess how
badly we messed up and thank Him for putting up with us.
And in that moment, upon hearing that pain and remorse, God
speaks to our giant fish and suddenly we are free, back in His
light! How wonderful to be on God's dry land.

---

*Swallowed up within this world's darkness, I come to You—
my Lord of light—to tell You how, when, and where I
messed up. Thank You for putting up with my shenanigans.
Please help me find my way back into Your light!*

SIMPLE

*But he's already made it plain how to live, what to do, what GOD
is looking for in men and women. It's quite simple: Do what is fair
and just to your neighbor, be compassionate and loyal in your
love, and don't take yourself too seriously—take God seriously.*

MICAH 6:8 MSG

If we spent more time thinking about God than about ourselves,
our past, and our future, we'd live a lot more fully in the present.
After all, there's nothing we can do about the past. It can't be
changed. And there's no point worrying about the future. It isn't
here yet. Our time would be better spent living in the present
with the Presence—and living it His way, with justice, love, compassion, and a good sense of humor.

---

*Help me, Lord, to be fair and to be full of compassion and
love for my neighbor. Above all, Lord, don't let me get caught
in the trap of the should'ves, could'ves, and would'ves
of life. Help me live in the present, in Your Presence.*

NO MATTER WHAT

*The Lord is good, a Strength and Stronghold in the
day of trouble; He knows (recognizes, has knowledge of,
and understands) those who take refuge and trust in Him.*

Nahum 1:7 AMPC

God knows exactly what we are all about. He totally sees us for who
we truly are. And He still loves us. He still wants to and is ready to
take care of us when we run into trouble. So, if things are looking
bleak, a plan backfired and you're in a tough spot, don't despair.
Don't be afraid to approach God and run beneath His wing. He
gets it. He gets you. And He's ready to take you in—no matter what.

---

*Sometimes I can't get over the idea that, despite all
my mistakes, faults, and wrong turns, You still love
me, Lord. For that and so much more, I thank You as
I take refuge beneath Your wings once more.*

CLIMBING HIGHER AND HIGHER

The Lord God is my Strength, my personal bravery, and my
invincible army; He makes my feet like hinds' feet and will
make me to walk [not to stand still in terror, but to walk]
and make [spiritual] progress upon my high places.
HABAKKUK 3:19 AMPC

What a wonderful life a Christian woman has. You have God as
your strength, a veritable spiritual army that will come to your
aid at any moment you need Him. Because of Him, you are agile
enough to walk where no woman has gone before. Because of
Him, you don't fear anything. You will never be a deer caught in
the headlights but one that continues to climb higher and higher,
ever closer to God. That's something to celebrate!

You, Lord, are my strength, song, and rescuer. You come on
the run just when I need You. Help me, Lord, to walk where
You would have me walk, to go where no woman has gone
before. . .full of courage and hope, moving ever closer to You.

OH, WHAT A SAVIOR!

"For the LORD your God is living among you. He is a mighty savior.
He will take delight in you with gladness. With his love, he will
calm all your fears. He will rejoice over you with joyful songs."
ZEPHANIAH 3:17 NLT

What a way to start the day! Planting firmly into the soil of your mind, body, and soul that God is living among us. That the one who saved you, Jesus, delights in you. He's tickled pink that you are in His life! Wrapped in His arms, He gives you the peace only He can give. He is so happy with you that He can't help but burst out in song. He's more than a Savior—He's what you can't live without! So rejoice in the Lord today and watch it spill over onto others. That Jesus joy—it's contagious!

Wrap Your arms around me, Lord, as I come before You
today. With Your love, calm all my fears. Allow me to rest
my head upon Your chest, aligning each breath with Yours.
Sing Your words of love and delight into my waiting ears.

ENERGY SOURCE

" 'Get to work! For I am with you.' The GOD-of-the-Angel-
Armies is speaking! 'Put into action the word I covenanted
with you when you left Egypt. I'm living and breathing
among you right now. Don't be timid. Don't hold back.' "
HAGGAI 2:4–5 MSG

God has given each woman a special role to play or job to do in her time here on earth. Whether she be a housewife, a career woman, single, married, a mother, an evangelist, a writer, or a preacher, God is walking beside her right now. He is the main source of her energy. With that thought in her mind, she need not be shy but boldly follow the course God has laid out for her. Holding nothing back, she reveals herself to be a woman of God's strength!

I imagine You beside me, Lord, living and breathing.
With You on my side, I never need to fear and instead walk
boldly into this world, following Your commands, feeding off
Your energy, taking the path You would have me take, and
fulfilling the purpose for which You have designed me.

AN AWESOME HARVEST

"I will save you, and you shall be a blessing.
Do not fear, let your hands be strong."

ZECHARIAH 8:13 NKJV

How awesome to think that God has made you a blessing. Because you are a boon to others, He doesn't want you to be afraid of anything. Instead, God wants you to look around you. Take in everything and everyone. Where, amid all the ups and downs of this world, can you be a blessing to someone else, with or without her knowledge? Whose day can you make today? Whether it be through making food, donating money, or helping to rebuild someone's home, step out into the world. Be God's blessing. Sow your love and compassion, and reap an awesome harvest.

I want to be a blessing to others just as You have been a blessing to me, Lord. So give me the courage to do what You would have me do. Help me to sow my love and compassion into the life of others, just as You have sown Your love and compassion into me.

A FLOOD OF BLESSINGS

"Bring all the tithes into the storehouse so there will be enough food in my Temple. If you do," says the LORD of Heaven's Armies, "I will open the windows of heaven for you. I will pour out a blessing so great you won't have enough room to take it in! Try it! Put me to the test!"

MALACHI 3:10 NLT

Can you, daughter of God, imagine that just by giving God His due, He will more than double the investment of time and money you make to your church? And it won't just be a little drop of a return—but a flood of blessings that will come your way. Not sure it's true? Try it. It's God's promise. And you know He never lies! You can always count on Him and His blessings.

Train me, Lord, to bring my tithes of time and money into Your house. I want to be a blessing to You, just as You have been a blessing—and so much more!—to me. All glory and praise to You, my Lord, my God, my light!

COURAGEOUS

*"She will bring forth a Son, and you shall call His name Jesus,
for He will save His people from their sins."... "And they shall
call His name Immanuel," which is translated, "God with us."*

MATTHEW 1:21, 23 NKJV

Imagine an angel coming to your fiancé, telling him that you are
going to have a son and name Him Jesus, but everybody will call Him
Immanuel. Can you imagine being Mary, who had her own angel
bearing news? What amazing revelations for a young couple just
starting out! Fortunately for all of us, these two were no shirkers
of duty. Joseph valiantly protected Mary, and Mary bravely bore
the Savior into our world. Courage breeds courage. Ask God how
you too can be brave for Jesus, who walks with you today.

---

*I cannot imagine what Mary and Joseph went through.
But their courage as well as Your courage, Jesus, inspires
me to have courage of my own. Help me not to be a shirker
of duty but to walk forward in the world with boldness,
knowing You are with me each step of the way.*

TOUGH LOVE

"You have heard the law that says, 'Love your neighbor' and hate your enemy. But I say, love your enemies! Pray for those who persecute you!"
MATTHEW 5:43–44 NLT

When someone hurts us, it seems instinctual to hurt them right back. But Jesus would have us do just the opposite. Turning the other cheek seems especially tough for mothers, for nothing gets us more vengeful than someone who hurts our child—or any child for that matter. But what feels right instinctually is often not right spiritually. Shock your enemies by loving them. In doing so, you'll be imitating the God who loved us while *we* were still offenders. While you're at it, pray for your enemies. It may not change them for the better, but it will definitely change you.

I need help in the turning-the-other-cheek area, Lord. It's so easy to lash out when others lash out at me. But I know the path You would have me take, which is to love and pray for my enemies, to repay evil with good. Give me the strength and love to do so.

PRIVATE ROOM

*When you pray, go into your [most] private room, and, closing
the door, pray to your Father, Who is in secret; and your
Father, Who sees in secret, will reward you in the open.*

MATTHEW 6:6 AMPC

Sometimes it's hard for a busy woman to find any privacy, especially if she's got young kids. But how cool to know your "private room" for prayer doesn't have to be an actual room. It can be a mountaintop, desert, garden, or kitchen. Or it can be a place you envision in your mind while you sit in a pew, car, office, or train. What it's not to be is a platform where you impress other people with your overplayed oratory skills. It's simply a safe place where you go, within or without, and meet with God privately. That's a reward in itself.

---

*I come before You today, Lord, for some private time. I close
the door to the distractions around me and seek Your presence.
Here I am safe. Here I meet You. Here I am loved. Here I find the
peace I crave. Here I bring my requests, praises, and thanksgiving.*

FREE-FLUNG FORGIVENESS

"In prayer there is a connection between what God does and what you do. You can't get forgiveness from God, for instance, without also forgiving others. If you refuse to do your part, you cut yourself off from God's part."
MATTHEW 6:14–15 MSG

This thing about our forgiving others in order to be forgiven by God seems like a great challenge in this oftentimes dog-eat-dog society. But, as Christians, we are to travel a different road, one that seems illogical to the world around us. Because we are to love others as God loves us, we are also to forgive others as God has forgiven us. When we do so, we break the chain of "getting even," find true freedom with others and especially with God, and can rechannel our vengeful energy into more constructive areas. So heal the hostility. Break free with forgiveness. Fling yourself into love.

Help me, Lord, to remember I am to love others as You love me, to forgive as You forgive me. When I do, I can heal whatever hostility exists between me and others. In Your power, Lord, I'm ready to fling myself into love.

NOTHING ELSE NEEDED

"Where your treasure is, there your heart will be also."
MATTHEW 6:21 NKJV

Every once in a while, when we see the perfect purse, the most darling pair of shoes, or an absolute must-buy outfit, we women can literally break out in a cold sweat. But, really, how many purses, pairs of shoes, or changes of clothing does one woman need? And how long will they stay in style? Rather than focusing all our attention on keeping one step ahead of the Joneses and spending all our money on the latest fashions, God would have us focus on Him and spend our love, compassion, charity, and forgiveness on others. The treasures on earth are passing fancies. But the treasures in heaven, on all of God and His good things, are where our hearts should be. For nothing else is needed.

Too many times, Lord, I get caught up in obtaining more and more stuff in this material world. So I pray You would help me focus more on You and helping others than on what I can buy for myself. For You are all I truly need.

THE POWER OF PERSISTENCE

"Keep on asking, and you will receive what you ask for.
Keep on seeking, and you will find. Keep on knocking,
and the door will be opened to you. For everyone
who asks, receives. Everyone who seeks, finds. And to
everyone who knocks, the door will be opened."
MATTHEW 7:7–8 NLT

Women have many dreams—having the perfect career, finding the right man, becoming a mother, holding that first grandchild, and more. But sometimes we either forget to ask God about these things or we give up if we don't get our prayers answered overnight. God loves the persistence of His people. And each time we go to Him, our prayers morph into the prayers He wants us to pray. So keep asking, keep seeking, keep knocking. Don't give up. Your answer may be just around the corner and through the next door.

Let's face it, Lord. I live in a society that demands instant gratification. But You are from another world. You want us to be persistent, to continually ask You to satisfy our desires, to keep seeking an answer, to keep knocking until a door opens. Help me be a persistently seeking woman!

DETERMINED FAITH

She kept saying to herself, If I only touch His garment,
I shall be restored to health. Jesus turned around and,
seeing her, He said, Take courage, daughter! Your faith has
made you well. And at once the woman was restored to health.
MATTHEW 9:21–22 AMPC

Imagine bleeding for twelve years, then hearing about a man who could heal you. You get this thought stuck in your head: *If I just get close enough to touch Him, I will be made well.* It is this kind of faith that makes Jesus take notice. This woman with an issue of blood had no ifs, ands, or buts in her thoughts. She knew. She determined. She braved. And as a result was made whole once more. May you approach Jesus with your own such assurance and hear Him say, "Daughter, your faith has made you well."

Banish all the ifs, ands, and buts from my thoughts,
Lord. Transform my doubts into certainties. Make me a
determined woman of faith who approaches You with an
assurance and a courage that makes You take note.

GOD'S GREATEST TREASURE

Even the very hairs of your head are all numbered.
Fear not, then; you are of more value than many sparrows.
MATTHEW 10:30–31 AMPC

Women love it when someone notices and compliments them on their hair. So just imagine how fabulous it is that God not only notices each one of your hairs but actually has them all counted! On top of that, He truly values you—and what you say, think, do, believe. He's paying attention to your every thought, word, and worry. Although it may seem like you are a tiny cog in a big wheel, take heart in the fact that God knows and loves every intimate detail about you. You are so precious in His sight, there's no need to be afraid. So go forward today with faith and courage, knowing you are one of His greatest treasures.

In this world, Lord, we women can sometimes feel
like we're invisible—that what we say doesn't count,
doesn't matter, or isn't valued. But with You, it's different.
You truly care about what we say, think, do, and believe.
Thank You for making me feel treasured!

DIRECT CONNECTION

"I was hungry, and you fed me. I was thirsty, and you gave
me a drink. I was a stranger, and you invited me into your
home. I was naked, and you gave me clothing. I was sick,
and you cared for me. I was in prison, and you visited me."
MATTHEW 25:35–36 NLT

It's true that today's woman is busy with family, work, school,
home, and church and all the organizations that come with those
responsibilities. Yet God would have us serve an even greater
cause—reaching out a hand to the hungry, thirsty, stranger, naked,
sick, and imprisoned. By doing so, we are connecting directly
with Christ. For He can be found amid the overlooked, the ignored,
the abused who need our love and assistance. Look around you
today. Where can you find and serve Christ?

Open my eyes to the people around me, Lord. Help me
to notice those who are overlooked, ignored, abused—
those who need my love and assistance. Show me how I can
serve You by being a blessing to someone who needs one.

BECOMING A LANDSCAPER

"I tell you the truth, you can say to this mountain,
'May you be lifted up and thrown into the sea,' and
it will happen. But you must really believe it will
happen and have no doubt in your heart."
MARK 11:23 NLT

A woman often has a huge range of obstacles before her, so many that sometimes they can begin to weigh her down. Yet this is not so with a woman of faith, right? Jesus says straight out that you have the power to move those mountainous obstacles. How? By truly believing that you can. That means not one iota of doubt can be in your heart. Still not so sure? Then ask God to increase your faith as you daily pray His mountain-moving promise. Before you know it, you'll find yourself a tried-and-true landscaper!

Increase my faith, Lord. Help me to believe that I
can move mountains—that I can take an obstacle
and remove it from my path. Make me a woman who
believes with all her heart, strength, soul, and mind
that with You, the impossible is totally possible!

A CONDUIT OF LOVE

"The most important commandment is this: 'Listen,
O Israel! The LORD our God is the one and only LORD. And
you must love the LORD your God with all your heart, all
your soul, all your mind, and all your strength.' The second
is equally important: 'Love your neighbor as yourself.' "
MARK 12:29–31 NLT

Jesus has whittled down all the commandments and regulations into two simple rules: love God with all of your being and love others as yourself. It sounds really easy. And it is! Until you get out of bed. Then all your good intentions sometimes just fly right out the window. So how is a woman to cope? Go to God! Ask Him to constantly and consistently flood you with His love and allow His love to flow through you to others. Then rise to the challenge.

Your Word, Lord, tells me that the most important thing
for me is to love You with all my being. The second is
to love neighbors as I love myself. That's a lot of loving
going on. Help me to rise to the challenge, to allow
Your love to flow through me and into others.

THE CHRIST CONNECTION

Jesus came down with them and took His stand on a level spot.
. . . And all the multitude were seeking to touch Him, for healing
power was all the while going forth from Him and curing
them all [saving them from severe illnesses or calamities].
LUKE 6:17, 19 AMPC

Jesus is standing before you. On level ground He has taken His place and is waiting. All He needs is for you to meet Him where He stands, to reach out to Him, wanting to touch Him. For He knows what you need. His power is emanating from Him, looking for a woman to heal, to soothe, to hold. Reach out today. Feel His power. Hear His voice. Make that Christ connection. And the kingdom of God is yours!

Here I am, Lord, looking to be healed, soothed,
and held. In reaching out to You, I feel Your power
and hear Your voice. Here, in Your presence, I am
truly home, lingering in the love I crave.

A NEEDED DEED

*"What do you think? Which of the three became
a neighbor to the man attacked by robbers?"
"The one who treated him kindly," the religion scholar
responded. Jesus said, "Go and do the same."*
LUKE 10:36–37 MSG

After Jesus tells a scholar we are to love our neighbors as ourselves, the student asks for a definition of *neighbor*. Then Jesus goes on to tell the story of the Good Samaritan (see Luke 10: 25–37). As it turns out, the neighbor is whoever we see that needs help. It can be the people next door to your house, your pew, or your desk. It can be the woman in the park, on the subway, or at the mall. Instead of focusing on your smart phone, focus on Christ's command. Look up and all around you for that neighbor in need, and do your good deed.

---

*Help me to remove my self-focus. . .to ignore the distractions
of this world. . .to truly see with eyes of love, Lord. Show
me who I can help today. For by doing so, I become more
and more like You. And that's the supreme goal, right?*

SUCH LOVE

"This is how much God loved the world: He gave
his Son, his one and only Son. And this is why:
so that no one need be destroyed; by believing in him,
anyone can have a whole and lasting life."
JOHN 3:16 MSG

Imagine sacrificing your son, the one through whom your world was made, for the sake of others. Deserting Him at His greatest hour of need, just so that others could be saved. That's how much God loved the world. So that you would not be destroyed. How can you ever pay God back? By trusting in, clinging to Jesus. By making Him your all in all. By loving others as much as He loved you. By thanking Him for the gift of eternal life. By making each day count—for Him.

There's no way I can repay You for what You've done
for me, Lord. But what I can do is live the life You would
have me live by loving others as much as You love me;
by making each day count for You; by clinging to You.

TWO LITTLE WORDS

Jesus wept.

JOHN 11:35 NKJV

Although this verse—"Jesus wept"—is short, it still packs a punch. These two little words speak of Jesus' great compassion for people. And although this phrase is somewhat sad, it lifts us up. For this reminds us that Jesus knows exactly what we're going through in every phase of our life. He knows the pain, the strain, the stress of living in this world. He also knows the joy, the beauty, the love that surround us. He knows what it means to have a bad day, to grieve for a loss, to be betrayed, to be treated harshly, to not fit the norm. Thus, we are free to run to Him for any little thing. He's one man who will always listen. In fact, He is straining to hear from you. Talk to Him today. Tell Him all. He'll understand.

I come to You, Lord Jesus, into Your presence, looking for some peace and understanding. You know every range of human emotion. You know the stress of living an earthly life. So please listen to what I have to say. Then lean into me with all the love, comfort, and calm I crave.

AWESOME POWER

Suddenly, there was a bright light in the cell, and an angel of the Lord stood before Peter. The angel struck him on the side to awaken him and said, "Quick! Get up!" And the chains fell off his wrists.

ACTS 12:7 NLT

Prayer power is amazing! When fellow believers are praying with every part of their being, the world fills with light. Angels come to the rescue—even while we're sleeping! Our chains—of addiction, self-pity, unforgiveness, self-reliance, and so forth—just fall off. Next thing you know, we are walking, as if in a dream. We're outside. Free again! Once we come to our "senses," we realize the miracle of God's working in our life. So never give up! Do not surrender to doubt and fear. Keep on praying for yourself and others. Realize and prove the awesome power of prayer.

Too often, Lord, I see prayer as the last resort, but it should be the first thing I do when faced with a challenge. Help me not give in to doubt and fear but to keep praying for myself and others. Show me the miracles You're working in my life, Lord!

THE POWER OF PRAISE

But about midnight, as Paul and Silas were praying and singing hymns of praise to God, and the [other] prisoners were listening to them, suddenly there was a great earthquake.

ACTS 16:25–26 AMPC

Prayer is a super weapon. But so is singing hymns of praise to God! After all, when Paul and Silas prayed and sang after being beaten, thrown into a dungeon, and chained to the wall, a great earthquake shook the prison, opened all the doors, and unchained everyone! So, when you feel beaten down by life, a prisoner of problems, and fettered to your worries, try praying, then singing a song of praise. Before you know it, you'll be free. That's the power of praise!

I'm feeling beaten down today, Lord. I don't understand why what's happening is happening. So I'm coming to You, ready to pray and then praise. When I use these tools, I know I'll experience the power of You and Your angels working on my behalf!

EYES UP

Abraham was first named "father" and then became a
father because he dared to trust God to do what only God
could do: raise the dead to life, with a word make something
out of nothing. When everything was hopeless, Abraham
believed anyway, deciding to live not on the basis of what
he saw he couldn't do but on what God said he would do.

ROMANS 4:17–18 MSG

How wonderful to believe something just because God said so.
That's how Abraham realized the dream God had given him. He
knew God—who created the entire world—could, with one word,
"make something out of nothing." Are things looking hopeless to
you? Believe anyway. Keep your eyes on what God can do instead
of what you can't do. Oh daughter, dare to trust God! No matter
what, believe Him. And all your dreams *will* come true! That's His
promise!

Lord, I needed this word today! Thank You for reminding me
that I can't live according to what I think I can't do, but on the
basis of what You can do and said You will do! This truth makes
all the difference in my outlook. This truth gives me hope!

HIGH EXPECTATIONS

*This resurrection life you received from God is not
a timid, grave-tending life. It's adventurously expectant,
greeting God with a childlike "What's next, Papa?"*

ROMANS 8:15 MSG

This new life in Christ is awesome! Now that we're on board with what God wants for our lives, that He is with us every step of the way, we can be bold! Adventurers! Instead of cowering in fear, we are wonderfully courageous women, knowing that nothing can hurt us on this side of eternal life. We await God's orders with high expectations, and He leads us to more than we can imagine. One step at a time He takes us closer and closer to the prize set before us, as we, His daughters, continually ask, "Where to now, Abba?"

---

*Thank You, Lord, for being with me every step of the
way in my walk with You. Knowing that because You
are with me, nothing can truly hurt me, gives me the
courage to venture out, to follow You. . .to ask with
great anticipation, Where are we going today, Abba?*

THE INTERPRETER

*We don't know what God wants us to pray for. But the
Holy Spirit prays for us with groanings that cannot be
expressed in words. And the Father who knows all hearts
knows what the Spirit is saying, for the Spirit pleads
for us believers in harmony with God's own will.*

ROMANS 8:26–27 NLT

Our mother is ill, and we've become stressed-out caretakers. Our daughter is rebelling, and we don't know how to reach her. Our marriage is teetering, and we're not sure how to save it. Sometimes, we hardly know how to pray. But we feel an intense desire to lay our lives out before God, begging for His help. Fortunately, we have the Holy Spirit to interpret our groans, our sighs, our cries to God. So go to prayer, knowing that God will hear your heart and respond with exactly what you need.

---

*It's hard to put into words the troubles in my heart, Lord. But
knowing that Your Holy Spirit can translate my moans into words
comforts my soul. So here I am, Lord, coming to You in prayer,
lifting up my heart, knowing You'll respond with just what I need.*

ACCORDING TO PLAN

*We are assured and know that [God being a partner
in their labor] all things work together and are [fitting
into a plan] for good to and for those who love God and
are called according to [His] design and purpose.*

ROMANS 8:28 AMPC

What a relief knowing that what sometimes seems like a mish-mash of life is actually somehow all coming together. That all the decisions we've made, everything that's happened, need not be analyzed but seen as something God actually had planned for us. And that everything about this plan has not only made us what we are today but has worked well together for God's purpose. So no need looking back, really. And no need to worry about the future. Whatever is going to happen—be it good or bad—is all in God's hands. And that's the best place our lives can be.

---

*What a relief, Lord, that my life is in Your hands and whatever
happens is aligned with Your plan. This helps me let go of my
past, stop worrying about the future, and simply focus on
the present, where You are—and just where I want to be!*

ORIGINAL DESIGN

*Give your bodies to God because of all he has done for
you. . . . This is truly the way to worship him. Don't copy
the behavior and customs of this world, but let God
transform you into a new person by changing the way you
think. Then you will learn to know God's will for you.*
ROMANS 12:1–2 NLT

It's so easy to get caught up in this world's passions and pleasures.
Each day we're inundated by the media, being told we need this
or should want that. Yet, as Christians, we are to imitate Christ,
not the latest fashion model, starlet, or American idol. When you
accepted Christ, you began changing into who God originally
designed you to be. So don't stop now. Give yourself up to Him—
and only Him—each day. Let Him continue to transform you at
the core into the apple of His eye.

---

*I give myself up to You each day, Lord. I look to imitate Your Son,
Jesus, walking in Your will and way. I pray that every moment
You'd continue to transform me into the person You originally
created me to be—and find me a willing participant in the process.*

A WAY OUT

*The temptations in your life are no different from what
others experience. And God is faithful. He will not allow the
temptation to be more than you can stand. When you are
tempted, he will show you a way out so that you can endure.*

1 CORINTHIANS 10:13 NLT

Women often face a myriad of temptations whether we're being
enticed to buy an item we really can't afford, eat a second bowl
of ice cream, or scarf down a chocolate Easter bunny originally
bought for the kids. In each of those circumstances, God shows us
a way out, an escape route. Our job is to actually look for the EXIT
sign. So before buying that new dress or adding another inch to
your hips, take a deep breath and look for God. He's waving you
toward the exit ramp.

---

*When a temptation comes my way, Lord, I pray You'd open my
eyes to whatever escape route You've provided so I won't give in
or give out. When an enticement gets my attention, help me take
a deep breath and look for You waving me toward the exit ramp!*

FOREVER LOVE

Faith, hope, love abide [faith—conviction and belief respecting
man's relation to God and divine things; hope—joyful and
confident expectation of eternal salvation; love—true
affection for God and man, growing out of God's love for
and in us], these three; but the greatest of these is love.
1 CORINTHIANS 13:13 AMPC

Most women are drawn to romantic movies. There is something
so special and heartwarming about a man and a woman falling in
love. It piques our interest because we too love being in love. The
love we have for our man is special, but the love we have for and
from God is even more amazing. In fact, it's the greatest thing that
exists on heaven and earth. Yes, faith and hope will one day be realized by us in heaven, but God's love will endure forever and ever.

I truly adore You, Lord. You are the personification of love,
the most wondrous and delightful thing there is. Help me to
make time for You in my life, Lord. To listen when You speak,
to walk where You will, to love You more and more each day.

E FOR EFFORT

Be firm (steadfast), immovable, always abounding in the
work of the Lord [always being superior, excelling, doing
more than enough in the service of the Lord], knowing
and being continually aware that your labor in the Lord
is not futile [it is never wasted or to no purpose].
1 CORINTHIANS 15:58 AMPC

Some Sundays when we show up to teach adult Sunday school, our classroom is empty. Turns out everyone went to the firehouse breakfast. Other days we come with all our craft supplies for kids' church, and all the children are home with the flu. When these things happen, we may feel as if our effort has been wasted. But anything and everything we do for the Lord has a purpose. So keep up the good work, ladies. God sees what you're doing and is finding a way to use it for His good.

Thank You, Lord, for taking whatever human effort I expend
and using it for Your good. Help me remember that my work
is never wasted. May all I do be worthy and lovely in Your
sight and used for Your purposes on earth and in heaven.

CHAIN OF COMFORT

God is our merciful Father and the source of all comfort.
He comforts us in all our troubles so that we can
comfort others. When they are troubled, we will be able
to give them the same comfort God has given us.
2 CORINTHIANS 1:3–4 NLT

When we suffer the death of a loved one, we almost feel as if we will never see daylight again. But then someone comes along, another woman who has suffered the same loss. She needn't say anything. Her very presence gives us peace, for we know she knows what we feel. It's a chain of comfort: from God, to another, to us. When the darkness abates, when we heal once more, we see another woman bowed down with grief. We approach and the chain continues. What a comfort. What a woman. What a God. What links of love.

Thank You, Lord, for always being there to dry my eyes,
to wrap a reassuring arm around me, to remind me
that no matter what losses I suffer, I will always have
You. In turn, Lord, help me be a conduit of Your comfort
by extending to others what You've given me.

EYES OF FAITH

*We walk by faith [we regulate our lives and conduct
ourselves by our conviction or belief respecting man's
relationship to God and divine things, with trust and holy
fervor; thus we walk] not by sight or appearance.*

2 CORINTHIANS 5:7 AMPC

There are those who believe we are born, live, die, and that's it.
Once the physical world is gone, there is only emptiness. Yet those
of us who believe in things that we cannot see—God the Father,
Jesus the Son, and the Holy Spirit—know there is so much more.
This is what gives us hope. After all, gravity exists and cannot be
seen. The same can be said of love, which is not only invisible but
eternal. Ladies, keep your eyes of faith on the divine and you will
never, ever walk or live alone—on earth or in heaven.

*My eyes are on You, Lord, as I step each day along this walk
of faith. Your existence gives me the hope I need to carry on.
By focusing on You, I know I'll never be alone or abandoned—
on earth or in heaven. All praise and thanks to You!*

MAJOR DO-OVER

This means that anyone who belongs to Christ has become
a new person. The old life is gone; a new life has begun!
2 CORINTHIANS 5:17 NLT

Life doesn't offer us many do-overs. Yet all who believe in Christ
get a major one—an entire life do-over! When we begin to believe,
when we get serious about our faith, when we graft ourselves onto
the Christ tree, an amazing transformation occurs. We become
brand new. We become empowered by the greatest force on heaven
and earth—love! Every step we take is on the new road to freedom
in Christ, the one who forever changed the world. We go from
caterpillar to butterfly, never to crawl again. Instead, we take
flight, soar between heaven and earth, forever transformed.

Thank You, Lord, for making me a new woman. Grafted
onto You, I have become brand new. Talk about an extreme
makeover! In You and with You, I am transformed from a
caterpillar to a butterfly, ready and willing to soar with You!

MINDING MENTAL MEANDERINGS

We lead every thought and purpose away captive into the
obedience of Christ (the Messiah, the Anointed One).
2 CORINTHIANS 10:5 AMPC

Thoughts can be wild things. From concerns about children, to worries about job loss, to fears about finances, your mental meanderings can really bring you down. They can keep you from seeing with the eyes of faith. So blinded, you may find yourself groping your way through life—afraid, suspicious, worried, haunted, trapped. So don't let your thoughts run wild. Pay attention to what you are saying to yourself. Ever alert, endeavor to replace negative thoughts with uplifting, God-healing scripture. For memorizing Bible verses will do a woman's mind—and body—nothing but good. And 2 Corinthians 10:5, the verse above, is a great place to start as you begin minding your mental meanderings.

Help me rein in my thoughts, Lord, when they start
careening out of control and away from You. Open my
mind with Your Word so I see with eyes of faith.

EVER-EXPANDING RETURN

Let's not allow ourselves to get fatigued doing good.
At the right time we will harvest a good crop if we don't
give up, or quit. Right now, therefore, every time we get
the chance, let us work for the benefit of all, starting with
the people closest to us in the community of faith.

GALATIANS 6:9 MSG

With so many opportunities to do good in this world, women, natural-born nurturers, may feel as if it's a losing battle. How will we ever accomplish all that needs to be done? Well, we needn't worry. If we all just keep helping, beginning with those at home and at church, we'll eventually reap a good harvest. So simply keep nurturing where you naturally can, confident that everything will come out right for you and the lives of those you touch, remembering that tender loving care tends to yield an ever-expanding return.

There's so much darkness and evil in the world, Lord,
that doing good can be exhausting. But because
You're in my life, I know I have the power to continue
working for the benefit of all, each and every day!
For one day we'll reap a glorious harvest—for You!

MASTER'S PLAN

We are God's [own] handiwork (His workmanship), recreated in Christ Jesus, [born anew] that we may do those good works which God predestined (planned beforehand) for us [taking paths which He prepared ahead of time], that we should walk in them [living the good life which He prearranged and made ready for us to live].
EPHESIANS 2:10 AMPC

Women love to have a plan. It makes us feel secure, almost as if we are in control. So how great is it that when we are born again in Christ, we are able to begin doing the things God planned way back. We begin walking on paths He's already laid out for us. We begin having the life He wanted us to have. That Master's plan— a relief and an adventure at the same time! Walk on, ladies! Walk on!

Lord, I think it's so cool that You have such wonderful plans for me—that I am already walking on the path You have laid out for me. Be with me, Lord, as I walk through life beside You, my favorite and most beloved travel guide!

EMPOWERED BY GOD

I pray that from his glorious, unlimited resources he
will empower you with inner strength through his
Spirit. . . . Now all glory to God, who is able, through
his mighty power at work within us, to accomplish
infinitely more than we might ask or think.

EPHESIANS 3:16, 20 NLT

When we bow down to Christ, laying aside our weakness, we rise in His power within, stronger than we ever have been before. Through us, God works miracles. We suddenly find ourselves accomplishing something we never thought possible. Something beyond our imagination and understanding. Secure in His love, dreams begin coming true. It's time to stretch, ladies. Reach high! And witness the miracle of God's power within taking form without.

Lord, I lay aside my weakness as I bow down to You. I pray You
will work through me to do more than I ever thought or imagined
I would—or could—do. Give me the confidence to reach high,
secure in Your love and ready for my dreams to become reality!

GOOD MORNING, GOD!

Be constantly renewed in the spirit of your mind [having a fresh mental and spiritual attitude], and put on the new nature (the regenerate self) created in God's image.
EPHESIANS 4:23–24 AMPC

Each new day gives us a chance to make a fresh start, spiritually and mentally. And a great way to start that new day is by greeting God with a smile, a praise, and a prayer. Try this: Each morning, jump out of bed, and say, *"Good* morning, God!" Then greet Jesus and the Holy Spirit the same way. Acknowledge aloud that you know they will be with you, helping you to do all you have been called that day to do. Thank God for all your blessings—past, present, and future. Set out knowing that the three-in-one God is *with* you and going to do amazing things *through* you.

Good morning, God! Good morning, Jesus! Good morning, Spirit! Thank You for this new day! Thank You for walking with me, helping me do all I am called to do. Thank You for all my blessings. Everybody ready? Let's go!

145

SHARPEST TOOLS

Take the sword of the Spirit, which is the word of God.
Pray in the Spirit at all times and on every occasion. Stay alert
and be persistent in your prayers for all believers everywhere.
EPHESIANS 6:17–18 NLT

The sharpest tools in our spiritual shed are God's Word and our prayers. When we wield them, nothing can defeat us. When we use them, no weed can choke out our good intentions. To keep God's Word sharp, we need to study it, memorize it, believe it, and apply it to our lives. To keep our prayers on point, we need to speak to God daily and have a praise-filled attitude from sunup to sundown. In a constant state of prayer and praise, with God's Word recited back to Him, nothing can defeat His women, armed with the sharpest tools in God's shed.

Lead me through Your Word today, Lord. Show me what
You would have me write upon my heart and apply to my life.
Prompt me throughout this day to pray in the Spirit for all
people and all situations and to praise You over and over again!

THE HEART OF THE MATTER

I pray that your love will overflow more and more, and that
you will keep on growing in knowledge and understanding.
For I want you to understand what really matters.
PHILIPPIANS 1:9–10 NLT

It's amazing how one kind word can totally lift the spirit, how a simple smile can change a person's day, how five minutes of considerate and thoughtful listening can relieve another's burden. The more you learn about and understand God, the more you realize what is really important—you loving God and others. As you spend time in His presence, He fills you with His eternal love, which cannot help but spill over onto others. Your job: let it flow out and touch someone. Who can you encourage with a kind word? To whom can you lift a simple smile? For whom can you lend a listening ear? Go forward in love today.

Lord, fill me with Your love until it's overflowing.
Then, as I go through my day, help me to open my heart
and let that eternal love flow from me and touch the life
of another. Be with me as I move forward in love today.

A WOMAN EMPOWERED

*[For my determined purpose is] that I may know Him [that I may
progressively become more deeply and intimately acquainted
with Him, perceiving and recognizing and understanding the
wonders of His Person more strongly and more clearly], and
that I may in that same way come to know the power outflowing
from His resurrection [which it exerts over believers].*

PHILIPPIANS 3:10 AMPC

Wow! Resurrection power. The love Jesus poured out for us on the
cross, the love that raised Him from the dead for our sakes, that's
some pretty strong stuff. And it's available to you each and every
moment of every day. If you make it your aim and purpose to fully
believe in Jesus, to study Him, to walk in His steps His way, you too
will know His amazing strength. You will be a woman empowered
by God, a woman to be reckoned with.

---

*Fill me with Your resurrection love today, Lord. Remind me
that Your power is available to me every moment. Lead me by
Your Spirit as I walk in Your steps. Fill me with Your amazing
strength, and make me a woman of God to be reckoned with.*

WISE AHEAD

I press on to possess that perfection for which Christ Jesus
first possessed me. No, dear brothers and sisters, I have
not achieved it, but I focus on this one thing: Forgetting
the past and looking forward to what lies ahead.
PHILIPPIANS 3:12–13 NLT

Ah, forgetting the past. If only. But, yet, it's obviously possible. The apostle Paul did it. So can you! And although it may be something you have to do every day, that's okay too! When something you regret or cannot forgive enters your mind, tell it to take off, go away. You aren't going to waste your energy on what you can't change. You're wiser than that. Instead of mooning over the could've-should've-would'ves, you're going to use all your power to go forward. Good move!

Too often I find myself stuck in the past, Lord, replaying a tired
old scene—one I can't go back and change—over and over in
my mind. Help me to forget what's over and done. Give me the
wisdom to stop looking back and instead move forward in You.

NO BETTER WAY

Rejoice in the Lord always. I will say it again: Rejoice!
PHILIPPIANS 4:4 NIV

Yesterday may not have gone as well as you'd hoped it would. And today looks like it's shaping up to be another tough one. Energy is lagging. Hope isn't where it usually is. Everything just seems a little off. But wait. There's something you can do to change all of this: Rejoice in the Lord! Sing a song of praise. Get out that old hymnal, or grab the iPod and cue up some great contemporary Christian music. Start dancing with the Lord. Take joy in each and every move you make. He is with you! He is your very own! He loves you with all of His heart! He sees you as the apple of His eye! Rejoice in the Lord! Yes, rejoice! There's no better way to live!

Lord, I'm coming to You, singing a praise song at the top of my lungs. I'm going to start dancing, moving to the beat I find in Your love. Thank You, Lord God, for loving me in this life—for filling me with joy in every single step!

A TRUE LADY

Let your gentleness be evident to all. The Lord is near.
PHILIPPIANS 4:5 NIV

The word *gentlewoman* is hardly used at all anymore. Yet being called such is a wonderful compliment to any woman. It implies that you come from a good family and have good breeding. That you are a true *lady* in every sense of the word. But of *course* you come from a good family—you are God's daughter, the daughter of a King! A royal princess. There is no longer any need to be power hungry, to claw your way to the top—you are already there. You are indeed a gentlewoman—loving, kind, soft-spoken, selfless, Word-wise, comforting. And the best thing about it is that those who see the *gentle*woman so obvious in you know that God isn't very far behind.

Lord, thank You for reminding me that I don't have to claw my way to the top—because I'm already there! I'm Your daughter, a princess. Help me to act the part, to be gentle, loving, kind, comforting, and Word-wise so that everyone will know I'm Yours and You're my Lord.

CALM IN CHRIST

Don't worry about anything; instead, pray about everything.
Tell God what you need, and thank him for all he has done.
Then you will experience God's peace, which exceeds
anything we can understand. His peace will guard
your hearts and minds as you live in Christ Jesus.
PHILIPPIANS 4:6–7 NLT

Got some things on your mind? Are they making your brow furrow, your stomach clench? If so, take them to God. Tell Him *everything*—and be specific! Don't leave anything out. Tell Him all your intentions, and ask Him to align them to His will. Most of all, praise Him for yesterday's blessings, those awaiting you today, and those in the future. Afterward, allow God to fill you with His peace. You'll be amazed at how relaxed you are, your heart and mind calm in Christ instead of churning in chaos.

Lord, my worries are a load I can't carry on my own,
so I'm dropping them at Your feet. Thank You for filling
me with Your peace and calm. Hear my voice as I praise
You for yesterday's blessings, the ones in my path today,
and those that will be on my doorstep tomorrow.

MIND FILL

You'll do best by filling your minds and meditating on things true, noble, reputable, authentic, compelling, gracious—the best, not the worst; the beautiful, not the ugly; things to praise, not things to curse.

PHILIPPIANS 4:8 MSG

Today's TV shows, computer games, movies, newspapers, and books all seem to have dark, dreary, menacing themes. It's enough to send even the most upbeat person into the lowest of funks. And when we are low, we have less energy to do God's work. What's the answer? Feed your mind with good things. Watch a Hallmark instead of a horror movie, read inspirational instead of murder-filled books. Praise instead of pout. Consistently stop and check your thoughts. If they're dark, throw some godly light on them. Make a list of your blessings and successes each and every day. Go for the positive—and that's what you'll get.

Lord, the dark side takes me down and leaves me drained. So I pray that You would help me stay on the lighter side of things. Help me exchange my negative thoughts for positive ones. Replace my words with Yours. Let's begin by naming the latest blessings...

MAKING DO

I have learned how to be content with whatever
I have. . . . And this same God who takes care of me
will supply all your needs from his glorious riches,
which have been given to us in Christ Jesus.
PHILIPPIANS 4:11, 19 NLT

Looking back over your life, chances are you were happiest during those times you had to "make do." You were filled with the joy of finding a dress for half off, getting a good deal on a child's desk at a thrift shop, or telling stories on Friday night instead of going to the movies. Each event was special in its own way because you were content with doing what you could with what you had. Know that the same God who gives you that wonder-filled sense of contentment will always supply you with all you really need—which, thank God, is more than enough!

You're a God with an abundant supply. So I'm done
worrying about what I lack in the moment or may
lack in the future. I'm changing things up so that I
focus only on what I have and celebrate the blessings
at hand! With You, I have all I need—and more!

SUPER-SPIRITUAL STRENGTH

*I have strength for all things in Christ Who empowers
me [I am ready for anything and equal to anything
through Him Who infuses inner strength into me;
I am self-sufficient in Christ's sufficiency].*

PHILIPPIANS 4:13 AMPC

Ever hear of women performing amazing physical feats of strength in order to save a loved one? There are reported cases of a mother lifting a car to save her son; and a daughter upending a car to save her dad. One woman fought off two bears to save her children, and two teenage sisters lifted a tractor to save their father! Amazing, right? Yet even more amazing is the super-*spiritual* strength you have in Christ. You are infused with it! It's coursing through your inner woman right now! No need to fear or fret about anything—Christ has powered you up to face everything! What a lift!

---

*I love this truth—I have strength for everything because You
empower me, Jesus. You and Your Spirit are coursing through
my inner being at this very moment. And so, I will neither fret
nor fear because I am a follower of You, my Lord Jesus!*

IN LIGHT AND LOVE

God rescued us from dead-end alleys and dark dungeons.
He's set us up in the kingdom of the Son he loves so
much, the Son who got us out of the pit we were in, got
rid of the sins we were doomed to keep repeating.
COLOSSIANS 1:13–14 MSG

Before coming to Christ, you may have been in some really dark places—spiritually and physically. But God has rescued you from those shadows. He has brought you into the light and love of His Son. You have been brought up and out of the abyss. You no longer do things that once made you disappointed in yourself. Each and every day you grow stronger, freer, happier. You are a princess now. Praise God, the King. Praise Christ, the Savior and Son. Go forward in the truth and power of His light and love.

Thank You, Lord Jesus, for rescuing me from the shadows
of this world and bringing me into Your light. In Your
presence, while soaking in the light of Your Word,
I find myself becoming stronger, happier, freer...
All praise and glory to You—the great Three-in-One!

FROM THE BEGINNING

Everything, absolutely everything, above and below,
visible and invisible, rank after rank after rank of angels—
everything got started in him and finds its purpose in
him. He was there before any of it came into existence
and holds it all together right up to this moment.
COLOSSIANS 1:15–16 MSG

Jesus was not only God made visible on earth. He was also the
beginning of everything that we see—and all that we don't see!
And it is in this amazing master craftsman, the Word come to
life, that we find our true purpose—to love God, ourselves, and
each other. And it is in this Son of God, who suffered and died
for us, that everything in this world is *still* being held together.
What power! What love! What a magnificent Savior! Praise Him
today for all that—and more—from beginning to end!

You are the one thing holding me together, Lord.
You are the Creator of everything visible and invisible
in this world. To You, I owe my all. Thank You for
loving me—from beginning to end and beyond!

SPIRITUAL OUTLOOK

Since you have been raised to new life with Christ,
set your sights on the realities of heaven, where Christ
sits in the place of honor at God's right hand. Think
about the things of heaven, not the things of earth.
COLOSSIANS 3:1–2 NLT

When you walk with your eyes focused on the ground before you, chances are you'll miss many things that are going on *around* you. But God wants your eyes on things above, focused on Him. He wants your eyes up, not down. Your thoughts on Him, not things of this earth. When you look at things from His heavenly point of view, your outlook on everything changes and, in turn, so do you. With this new vantage point, you see the true reality of this world. So, chin up, ladies. God's just waiting to catch your eye—and mind!

I need a new way of looking at things, Lord, because
my perception is out of whack. Help me keep my eyes
and mind on things above—things of Your world and
not mine. For then I will see the reality of what lies
before me and the truth of what lies within me.

THE NEW YOU

[You] have clothed yourselves with the new [spiritual self],
which is [ever in the process of being] renewed and remolded
into [fuller and more perfect knowledge upon] knowledge
after the image (the likeness) of Him Who created it.
COLOSSIANS 3:10 AMPC

The "new you" is looking pretty good. Each day you are being renewed within and without. You are getting closer and closer to bearing the image of Jesus. Your nature is gentler, kinder, wiser than it once was. You are more giving, patient, loving than before. Chances are you aren't perfect. But you are coming along nicely. Never beat yourself up because you're not where you yet want to be. Instead, praise God because of how far He has already brought you. Every day is a new day and a time to celebrate the new you.

I know I'm not perfect, Lord. And I know I'm not yet where
I want to be. But I also know that every day I get closer and
closer to the woman You envisioned me to be. Be with me as I
celebrate how far I've come—all to Your praise and glory!

GODLY AMBITION

Make it your goal to live a quiet life, minding your own business and working with your hands, just as we instructed you before. Then people who are not believers will respect the way you live, and you will not need to depend on others.
1 THESSALONIANS 4:11–12 NLT

Let's face it. People are watching you. Nonbelievers want to know if you have really been changed by Jesus, if you walk the talk. So are you keeping calm in all circumstances or are you panicking every time the stock market takes a dive? Are you keeping your nose out of the business of others or are you the neighborhood gossip? Are you doing something productive or are you simply idling? Remember: you may be the only Bible other people ever read.

Be with me, Lord, as I endeavor to live a quiet life, keeping my nose out of other people's business, lending a hand where needed, and taking care of myself and others as much as I am able. May people see You through me.

TO-DOS

Always try to do good to each other and to
all people. Always be joyful. Never stop praying.
Be thankful in all circumstances, for this is God's
will for you who belong to Christ Jesus.
1 THESSALONIANS 5:15–18 NLT

If everyone followed the guidelines presented in the above verses, this world would be a much better place. So why not try to follow these edicts, one day at a time? If you make that your intention at the beginning of each day, chances are you *will* change your part of the world, as well as change yourself. That's because all of these qualities you would work to imbue are those of Jesus. He was goodness and joy personified. He had a constant inner, and sometimes outer, dialogue with His Father. And when He thanked God, abundance followed. Yes, these verses would make a great "what would Jesus to-do" list.

Help me make it a habit to be good to all people, Lord.
To smile instead of grimace, to have a prayer continually
upon my lips. I thank You for everything. May my
following You in these ways change me and my world!

HE WILL DO IT

Faithful is He Who is calling you [to Himself]
and utterly trustworthy, and He will also do it
[fulfill His call by hallowing and keeping you].
1 THESSALONIANS 5:24 AMPC

Whatever task God gives you to do, He will give you the strength to do it. Whatever dream He plants in your heart, He will give you the means to realize it. Whatever promises He makes, He will come through on. To do otherwise would go against His nature. For He never lies. And the word He gives never comes back void. So have faith, woman, that you already have the ability to do what God has created you to do. Step out in confidence. And all dreams—those of yours and God's—will come true.

Sometimes I doubt myself and my abilities, Lord. Help me
change that. Remind me that You have already given
me the ability and confidence to do what You have called
me to do. Together we can make our dreams come true!

HEARTFELT PEACE

Do not become weary or lose heart in doing right [but continue in well-doing without weakening]. . . . Now may the Lord of peace Himself grant you His peace (the peace of His kingdom) at all times and in all ways [under all circumstances and conditions, whatever comes].
2 THESSALONIANS 3:13, 16 AMPC

Sometimes you may feel as if your godly efforts are getting you nowhere. For it seems as if wars are a perpetual evil, as well as bombings, shootings, kidnappings, molestations. . . . Yikes, the list goes on and on. But no matter how bad things seem, know that God is counting on women of the way to keep on keeping on. To continue doing their part in His kingdom. And that's all you really need to know. So, peace within and without, sister. Stay strong in love and the Lord.

When I think of all that's going on in this world, Lord, my heart sinks. But I know that if I keep doing right, at least I'll be putting some good out into a world that really needs it. It's that truth that will keep me going strong and experiencing Your peace!

YOUR SPECIAL GIFT

*Do not neglect the gift which is in you, [that
special inward endowment] which was directly
imparted to you [by the Holy Spirit].*
1 TIMOTHY 4:14 AMPC

Lady, you are special. God has made you that way. Within you is a
gift no one else has. Have you discovered it yet? If so, are you using it
to bring others to God, to somehow awaken them to His presence?
For that's what your gift is there for. If you haven't yet discovered
your unique gift—which may be singing, teaching, preaching,
writing, painting, and so forth—spend some time in prayer. Ask
God to reveal your special talent to you. Don't wait another day.
Who knows but that you and your gift have come for such a time
as this—and there's not a moment to lose!

---

*Help me to use my gift for Your glory, Lord. Give me the
confidence to step into the area for which You have designed me.
When I have doubts, reveal my special talents. Then bless me
with the assurance to use my special gift for such a time as this!*

THE RIGHT PATH

Lust for money brings trouble and nothing but trouble.
Going down that path, some lose their footing in the faith
completely and live to regret it bitterly ever after.
1 TIMOTHY 6:10 MSG

Most people seem to know that they can't take anything with them when they leave this world. Yet it doesn't stop the majority of the population from worshipping the almighty dollar. Although money has its place—to keep us sheltered, warm, dry, clothed, and fed—it should in no way take the place of God. Unfortunately, some people learn that lesson the hard way. Save yourself the pain. Keep money off the altar of your heart. Stand strong in your faith. Keep God on His throne and you won't be thrown off the right path.

There are times, Lord, when I maybe don't lust for money but count on it more than I should. Help me to keep money from being my primary focus. Give me the faith to stand strong—keeping You on the throne of my heart and my feet walking Your way.

THREE SPIRITS

*For God did not give us a spirit of timidity (of cowardice,
of craven and cringing and fawning fear), but [He has
given us a spirit] of power and of love and of calm and
well-balanced mind and discipline and self-control.*
2 TIMOTHY 1:7 AMPC

In this world there are plenty of things to be timid and afraid of—
spiders, snakes, bats, dark alleys, violent storms—just to name
a few. But thank God that He has equipped us with three other
spirits—those of power, love, and self-control. That's an extremely
effective arsenal. With these spirits in your pocket and your
eyes on Christ, all worry, doubt, and fear dissipate. Next thing you
know, you're walking on the very waters that caused you concern
just moments before. And Christ is right there with you.

*Sometimes, Lord, I forget that You've equipped me with
power, love, and self-control. Help me to keep that truth
at the forefront of my mind so that, with my eyes on
You, all my worry, doubt, and fear will vanish.*

YOUR ROAD MAP

All Scripture is inspired by God and is useful to teach us what is true and to make us realize what is wrong in our lives. It corrects us when we are wrong and teaches us to do what is right.

2 TIMOTHY 3:16 NLT

The Bible—what a font of wisdom and instruction. The Old Testament stories are filled with life lessons of fellow flawed beings and believers of God. The Psalms contain songs that speak to human hearts, giving voice to sorrows and joys, fears and courage, frustration and success. The Proverbs overflow with practical wisdom. And the New Testament shows believers how to be like Christ. All that God has written is meant to help you find your way. It's your road map to heaven on earth. No GPS needed. Simply unfold the Word and allow it to enfold you.

Lord, I am so thankful for Your Word. I love the Old Testament stories of people who were as flawed as I am. The words of the Psalms reveal my true heart; the wisdom of the Proverbs feeds my mind; and the New Testament provides a road map to You. What more could I ask for?

GOOD ATTITUDE

Everything is pure to those whose hearts are pure. But nothing is pure to those who are corrupt and unbelieving, because their minds and consciences are corrupted. Such people claim they know God, but they deny him by the way they live.
TITUS 1:15–16 NLT

Nonbelievers seem to have a negative attitude about lots of things. They sometimes claim a belief in God when they're in trouble but then quickly deny, ignore, or insult Him when things are going well. Those whose hearts have been tainted see trouble everywhere. But believers in Christ, because they are filled with God's Word, have purer minds and consciences. Everything they see, as God said in the beginning, is "good." And with this attitude, their thoughts rise higher and higher. So, stay lifted and pure in heart and mind. Live in the Word—night and day. Witness the Light.

Remind me today, Lord, of all the good in the world. Help me keep my eyes on the myriad of blessings that surrounds me. Give me a mind with thoughts that rise higher and higher, closer and closer to You.

INSIDE OUT

I didn't want to do anything without your consent.
I wanted you to help because you were
willing, not because you were forced.

PHILEMON 14 NLT

God never really forces anything. If we are to believe Him, we are to do so willingly, not because He insists upon it. It's all about free will. We are free to believe or disbelieve. We are free to do good or not do good. Everything must come from our heart. That's what makes God so easy to love. If you are serving God in a way that's not from your heart, maybe it's time to step back and see where you might serve Him more compassionately. For when you mix your willing service with love, as Jesus did, amazing things begin to happen—from the inside out!

Show me, Lord, how to mix service with love. Help me
to do as You did, to speak as You did, to love as You did. . .
I want to do my part to share You with the world. Show
me how to serve, where to serve, who to serve. . .

HE KNOWS, SO GO

This High Priest of ours understands our weaknesses, for he faced all of the same testings we do, yet he did not sin. So let us come boldly to the throne of our gracious God. There we will receive his mercy, and we will find grace to help us when we need it most.
HEBREWS 4:15–16 NLT

How awesome to have Jesus, a High Priest who knows *exactly* what we're going through. He's actually walked this earth, breathed the same air we breathe. He knew grief at the death of a friend. He experienced abandonment by His followers and His Father. He knew the physical pain and emotional humiliation of a beating. He knew what it was like to be hated, spied on, and betrayed. Jesus is almost too familiar with what you are going through. So go to Him. He understands and is more than ready to help.

Lord, You're familiar with everything I'm going through. And so, I come to You in this moment, seeking Your grace, mercy, understanding, and compassion. Love me right where I am. Help me see this through. Help me to feel Your presence, to absorb Your healing, to know I am not alone.

NO DOUBT

Now faith is the assurance of things hoped
for, the conviction of things not seen.
HEBREWS 11:1 NASB

This verse is so short yet so powerful. It's part of an introduction to a list of heroes of our faith, only two of whose names are women. The first, Sarah, believed that God would make her a mother even though she was well past childbearing age. God promised; she believed. The second, the harlot Rahab, having heard about all the God of Israel had done, welcomed Joshua's spies. Because she believed their God was the one true God, capable of doing anything and everything, she was saved when the walls of Jericho fell—*and* she became an ancestress of Jesus! What a testimony of faith for women today. Go forward, believing, as Sarah and Rahab did. No longer doubt the impossible, but be assured your hopes will one day become your reality!

Lord, You give me the hope I need to live this life. In You,
I will go forward in faith, no longer doubting the impossible.
You have the power to transform my hopes into reality!

FAITHFUL FOLLOWER

Without faith it is impossible to please and be satisfactory
to Him. For whoever would come near to God must
[necessarily] believe that God exists and that He is the rewarder
of those who earnestly and diligently seek Him [out].
HEBREWS 11:6 AMPC

Are you constantly looking over your shoulder, trying to figure
out if you're on the right path? Do you get easily distracted and
forget to watch out to see where God may be leading you? Are you
continually second-guessing His plans for your life? If so, God
may be getting tired of you dragging your feet. Want to get somewhere great? Want to really please God? Gird up your faith. Believe
that God is with you and leading you! Look for Him everywhere!
Know that He has a great plan for your life—and that your only
job is to be a willing, diligent, faithful follower.

Thank You, Lord, for being with me, leading me, pointing out
the way You would have me go. Open my spiritual eyes to Your
constant presence. Guide me through Your plan for my life!

A FAMILIAR GUIDE

[Urged on] by faith Abraham, when he was called, obeyed and went forth to a place which he was destined to receive as an inheritance; and he went, although he did not know or trouble his mind about where he was to go.

HEBREWS 11:8 AMPC

Like He had for Abraham, God has a destination for you, a place He's leading you to. But you can forget about the earthly road map. Don't even begin charging your GPS. Just follow God, and He'll lead you to where you are meant to be. Like Abraham, may you be so obedient that you don't even bother thinking about where you're headed. May your faith be as solid as Abraham's, who, although he was unfamiliar with the landscape, was *totally* familiar with his guide. So, don't worry. Just go. Just believe. God will get you to where you are meant to be!

I want the faith of Abraham, Lord. I want to willingly and determinedly go where You lead, not worrying about the route or destination. May my knowledge of who You are give me the assurance that You will get me where You want me to go.

HOLD ON!

Be satisfied with your present [circumstances and with what you have]; for He [God] Himself has said, I will not in any way fail you nor give you up nor leave you without support. [I will] not, [I will] not, [I will] not in any degree leave you helpless nor forsake nor let [you] down (relax My hold on you)! [Assuredly not!]
HEBREWS 13:5 AMPC

The Amplified Bible really does this verse up. In interpreting the original language this verse was written in, you really get the point that God is definitely always going to be there for you. There is no way He's going anywhere without you. He's got you in His hand and will never, ever release His grip on you. So don't worry about whatever may be going on in your life. It's temporary. He's leading you to better days ahead. So just hold on!

Lord, I love how You have vehemently promised that You will never fail me, give me up, or leave me without Your support. The truth that You will never relax Your hold on me fills me with the confidence I need to keep going. . .in You!

LASTING REFUGE

So we take comfort and are encouraged and confidently and
boldly say, The Lord is my Helper; I will not be seized with alarm
[I will not fear or dread or be terrified]. What can man do to me?
HEBREWS 13:6 AMPC

Getting stressed out? Wondering where the next dollar is going to
come from or where the next madman with a gun or a bomb will
strike? How about this violent weather? Are you safe anywhere
these days? Yep! There's one place of refuge left—God. In Him,
there is no need to be panicked about anything. Nothing here on
earth can touch your soul or spirit. No one can tear you from God's
hands. So get confident. Get bold. Don't worry. You're in the right
place—God's arms.

I crawl into Your comforting arms, Lord. Wrap Your loving
presence around me. Never let me go. Remind me that I need
not ever be afraid. Because with You, I have everything and
am just where You would have me be—wrapped up in You.

GOD'S COURSE

If you need wisdom, ask our generous God, and he will
give it to you. . . . But when you ask him, be sure that
your faith is in God alone. Do not waver, for a person
with divided loyalty is as unsettled as a wave of the
sea that is blown and tossed by the wind. Such people
should not expect to receive anything from the Lord.

JAMES 1:5–7 NLT

Everyone needs wisdom at some time or another. And how great
that you can go to God and ask Him for it. The only thing is, you
must be confident that He will give you the answer you need. Once
you get on God's course, there's to be no going back, no taking
another route later due to uncertainty. Instead, be steady. Full
steam ahead. And God will get you where you need to go.

Sometimes, Lord, I feel untethered, distracted, unsure as to where
You'd have me be. . .where You'd have me go. And so, I'm coming
to You for reassurance, for strength, for wisdom, knowing that
if my faith is in You, I'll receive all I need to stay the course.

TRUE MOTIVES

You don't have what you want because you don't ask God for it.
And even when you ask, you don't get it because your motives
are all wrong—you want only what will give you pleasure.
JAMES 4:2–3 NLT

God, the ultimate provider, is ready to give you whatever you want.
Your only job is to ask Him for it. Like a child going to a parent, you
are to go to God and lay your desire before Him. If you are asking
with pure motives, you are sure to have your request granted. If you
are asking for something with the wrong motives, He'll probably
say no. So before asking God for anything, look deep within and
determine your true motives. And know that whatever His answer
is, He's doing what's best for you. That's what makes Him such a
great Father! His motive is true love.

You, Lord, are my ultimate provider. You have promised
to give me what's best for me. So help me search within
my heart for what I truly desire. Help me align my
hopes and dreams with the plans You have for me.

PRAYER POWER

The earnest (heartfelt, continued) prayer of a righteous man
makes tremendous power available [dynamic in its working].
JAMES 5:16 AMPC

When you are praying with your entire mind, soul, and spirit, when you are wholeheartedly coming before God, the heavens move. That's how much power prayer has! Imagine Elijah. He too was a mere mortal. Because of his heartfelt prayer, there was no rain for three and a half years. Then he prayed again, and it poured. (See James 5:17–18.) So, know, believe, have faith that there is power in folded hands. Go deep with each prayer. Focus all your attention on God, His Word, His power, and your request. Let your words and thoughts unfold before your almighty God. Move mountains with your faith.

Lord, I believe You've blessed Your people with the gift
of prayer—that there's power when I clasp my hands
together. Lord, help me move mountains with my faith
as I unfold my thoughts and lift my prayer to You!

FAITH LIFTS

Don't be concerned about the outward beauty of fancy
hairstyles, expensive jewelry, or beautiful clothes. You
should clothe yourselves instead with the beauty that
comes from within, the unfading beauty of a gentle
and quiet spirit, which is so precious to God.
1 PETER 3:3–4 NLT

When your inner beauty is shining forth, amazing things happen. Husbands disinterested in the whole "God thing" see something special in you and begin to thirst for a Savior. You become content with who you are. Worries cease. Your God-given gifts become evident and plentiful, bearing more and more fruit every day. Thus you become more of service to others. Your love for one and all becomes even more obvious. And, with God's help, you become a woman after His own heart. All from cultivating the beauty within! That's one awesome faith lift!

I want to become a woman after Your own heart, Lord.
So help me to be more focused on cultivating the light within
me. Show me how to allow my inner beauty to shine forth,
because I want to be more like Jesus in every way.

ALL READY

*God has given us everything we need for living a godly life.
... Because of [Christ's] glory and excellence, he has given
us great and precious promises. These are the promises
that enable you to share his divine nature and escape
the world's corruption caused by human desires.*

2 PETER 1:3–4 NLT

How cool that you are already equipped to become like Jesus. He has given you everything you need to be selfless, loving, compassionate, peaceful, faithful, wise, caring, patient, humble, and more! Because of all His promises, valued beyond compare, there is nothing stopping you from walking, talking, and living as Jesus did. The more you get to know Him through the Word and through prayer, the more like Him you will become. And that's a good thing!

*Lord, lead me in the ways that I can become more like
You. Show me who You are amid the events in my life.
Guide me to be more like You as I pray in this moment.*

REAL LOVE

Let's not just talk about love; let's practice real love.
This is the only way we'll know we're living truly, living
in God's reality. It's also the way to shut down debilitating
self-criticism.... For God is greater than our worried
hearts and knows more about us than we do ourselves.

1 JOHN 3:18–20 MSG

God *is* love. And love is the most powerful force on heaven and earth. It's greater than faith and hope. But it's not something just to be gabbing about. It's something to put out there each and every day, especially if you are a mother, wife, and friend. And it's not just about loving others. God wants you to love yourself as well. So stop that negative self-talk. See yourself for the precious princess you are in God's eyes. He knows more about you than you do. And He adores you.

I love You, Lord. Would You teach me how to love myself?
By seeing myself as a woman who's precious in Your
eyes, I know I will find a new way of loving others just as
You love me. It all comes full circle, doesn't it, Lord?

ACCORD

This is not a new commandment but simply a repetition of our original and basic charter: that we love each other. Love means following his commandments, and his unifying commandment is that you conduct your lives in love. This is the first thing you heard, and nothing has changed.

2 JOHN 5–6 MSG

Love is not just a mandate for outside the assembly of believers. The people in every Christian church are to love one another too. That means working together for the good of all. That means not holding grudges but putting others before you. That means not letting differences divide you. Instead, allow love, God's love, to unite you. Sing to the Lord a new song in accord, not discord. As much as you are able, live in love and peace with all. And God will smile on you and your church family.

May Your love change me, Lord. May it transform me into a woman who holds no grudges, a woman who seeks to unite all. And in that spirit of unity, Lord God, may I find the peace that holds and folds us all into You.

GOOD EXAMPLES

Dear friend, don't let this bad example influence you.
Follow only what is good. Remember that those who
do good prove that they are God's children, and those
who do evil prove that they do not know God.

3 JOHN 11 NLT

Even in the church, you may come across someone who rebels against the leadership, makes terrible accusations against others, and basically causes division. Such a person is setting a bad example—inside and outside of the church. If you yourself are ever in doubt of whose example to follow, look to Jesus. He is our best example of how to live a godly life. Follow in His footsteps, and you will never go down the wrong path. And, in so doing, you yourself will become a good example for others to follow.

Lord, help me to look for where You are walking. Help me
to follow in Your footsteps, embracing love, not hate; peace,
not discord; hope, not discouragement. Be my example,
my mentor, my guide in all ways for all my days.

TODAY'S BOOSTER

*You, dear friends, must build each other up in your most
holy faith, pray in the power of the Holy Spirit, and await the
mercy of our Lord Jesus Christ, who will bring you eternal
life. In this way, you will keep yourselves safe in God's love.*
JUDE 20–21 NLT

God loves those who encourage others, building people up instead
of tearing them down. One way to encourage people is by the
things you say. Another way is giving your support, whether it be
your money or helping hands. You can also encourage someone by
lifting her up in prayer. In all these ways you not only honor yourself and others but God and His love. So, who can you encourage?
Who needs your prayers? Who is desperate for godly love? Give
them a boost today.

*Help me watch my words, Lord. May I use them to build
others up, not tear them down. Show me who I can
encourage, pray for, love. . . . With Your help and guidance,
I know I can help to make this world a better place!*

THE OTHER SIDE

Behold, I stand at the door and knock; if anyone hears and listens to and heeds My voice and opens the door, I will come in to him and will eat with him, and he [will eat] with Me.

REVELATION 3:20 AMPC

Jesus is standing just outside, on the other side of the door. It's up to you to open it. Are you listening for His knock? If you are, and you open the door, He's going to come right in. He's ready to sit down with you, to talk things over, to clue you in, to break bread with you. How cool is that? So keep your ears open. Listen for Jesus' footsteps. When He knocks, let Him in. Let Him reveal His thoughts to you. It will be a dinner conversation you'll remember forever.

I feel so closed off today, Lord. Help me open my heart to Your presence, open my ears to Your voice, and open my mind to Your Word. In this moment, I invite You in. Let's sit down together and talk, just the two of us.

COMPLETE JOY

God will wipe away every tear from their eyes; and death
shall be no more, neither shall there be anguish (sorrow and
mourning) nor grief nor pain any more, for the old conditions
and the former order of things have passed away.
REVELATION 21:4 AMPC

Imagine how wonderful it will be when there are no more tears.
When there is no more pain and grief. When everything is totally
new. It may be hard to visualize, but it will happen. And, as a faithful
believer, one day you will be there. Until then, live with this vision,
this hope as you travel through life. Love everyone you meet. Pray
and praise continually. Know that every trial, temptation, and tear
is temporary. All of those things will one day pass. And on that
day, you will see Jesus in all His glory. And in that moment, your
joy will be complete.

I look forward to the day, Lord, when there will be no more
heartache, grief, or pain. Until then, I put all my hope in
You. I attempt to love everyone I meet. I praise You every
day. For in You and with You is where I find true joy.

SCRIPTURE INDEX